T0402276

Societal Self-empowerment in Germany

Peter Kirsch · Hanno Kube ·
Reimut Zohlnhöfer

Societal Self-empowerment in Germany

A Comparison of Fridays for Future and Corona Skepticism

Springer

Peter Kirsch
Abteilung Klinische Psychologie
Zentralinstitut für Seelische Gesundheit
Mannheim, Germany

Hanno Kube
Institut für Finanz- und Steuerrecht
Universität Heidelberg
Heidelberg, Baden-Württemberg,
Germany

Reimut Zohlnhöfer
Institut für Politische Wissenschaft
Universität Heidelberg
Heidelberg, Baden-Württemberg,
Germany

ISBN 978-3-658-40864-0   ISBN 978-3-658-40865-7   (eBook)
https://doi.org/10.1007/978-3-658-40865-7

This Springer imprint is published by the registered company Springer Fachmedien Wiesbaden
GmbH, part of Springer Nature.
The registered company address is: Abraham-Lincoln-Str. 46, 65189 Wiesbaden, Germany

Foreword

This book is the result of a joint project by the authors at the Marsilius Collegium of Heidelberg University, which we carried out as Fellows of the Collegium from 2020 to 2021. The starting point was the—often also publicly discussed—question of whether and, if so, to what extent people are increasingly taking the law into their own hands and disregarding applicable law and social conventions. When we designed our project in 2019, there was no talk of a worldwide pandemic, the consequent restrictions on our coexistence and the resulting social debate on the meaning and implementation of measures. At that time we thought of the school strikes by the Fridays-for-Future movement, but also of phenomena such as attacks on rescue services and municipal politicians or the actions of radical animal rights activists. Our goal was to describe, measure, explain and reflect on this behaviour, which we refer to as societal self-empowerment, and to consider how, if it is indeed a substantial problem, it can be countered. Then came the Corona pandemic and with it a form of societal self-empowerment that has given the topic a whole new dimension in terms of its visibility and presence in public discourse. Although we would have liked to do without the pandemic, it has opened up a field of research for us and for countless other scientists that is unique. In this way, we were able to study the dynamics of societal self-empowerment in times of crisis through a repeated representative survey and thus gain insights that would otherwise not have been possible. As a result, our project has gained even more significance and relevance and has received much more public attention than we originally expected. This is how the present book came about. We hope that you, dear reader, will find an interest in it and gain new insights from it.

At this point we would like to express our particular thanks to the Marsilius Collegium of Heidelberg University, which, through our Fellowship, has created opportunities that have made this project and the present publication possible in the first place. In particular, we would like to mention the Managing Director Tobias Just and the Directorate of the Collegium, Prof. Dr. Friederike Nüssel and Prof. Dr. Michael Boutros, who have followed our project with great benevolence and interest and supported it both financially and ideologically, not least through the financing of our surveys. We would also like to express our sincere thanks to the other Fellows of our class at the Collegium for the many helpful and enlightening discussions during our time there. We are indebted to Kathrin Ackermann, Fabian Engler, Frederic Kohlhepp, Marie Schliesser and Silja Wübbelmann for their comments on the questionnaire and on the text of this book and for their support in preparing the data and results.

Heidelberg   Peter Kirsch
in July 2022   Hanno Kube
                                                          Reimut Zohlnhöfer

Contents

Societal Self-Empowerment: Concept and Classification

1

Financial and debt crisis, refugee crisis, climate crisis, coronavirus pandemic, Ukraine war — we live in a time that seems to be determined by crises, worries and fears. In such a time, trust in established political and social institutions and procedures is strained. The people rightly ask whether these institutions and procedures are suitable and able to master the great crises and lead the country into a good future. Sometimes the trust seems to dwindle so much that individuals and groups begin to take the initiative back into their own hands and, in this sense, to empower themselves in order to express their discontent and to move things. An example are the Fridays for Future demonstrations that take place during school hours in order to emphasize the importance of the political issue and to attract attention. Another example are the Corona demonstrations, where regulations are deliberately disregarded. The same applies to break-ins in animal breeding operations, where violations of criminal law are accepted in order to document and make the suffering of the animals visible. The members of the "Last Generation" movement block roads to highlight the urgency of the issue of climate protection. And when municipal politicians are increasingly insulted and attacked physically in recent times, this too shows a form of self-empowerment that seems to be based on the loss of trust and dissatisfaction with the performance of the political system. How great and far-reaching the potential for possible self-empowerment is, becomes clear when one looks at groups such as the "Reich citizens", the "self-administrators" (prepping) and the followers of various conspiracy theories.

These initially diffuse, but at the same time clear findings were the starting point for the consideration to investigate the phenomenon of societal self-empowerment more closely with scientific methods in order to understand the phenomenon, to distinguish its problematic, but also its common good promoting dimensions and at the end possibly to be able to contribute to the question of which mechanisms social cohesion is based on.

P. Kirsch et al., *Societal Self-empowerment in Germany*, https://doi.org/10.1007/978-3-658-40865-7_1

Such an undertaking can only succeed interdisciplinarily from the outset. As far as coexistence in the community is structured by legal rules and is otherwise shaped by unwritten rules and conventions that are exceeded in the course of societal self-empowerment, legal science is addressed, whose area of inquiry is the binding rules of the community. Because self-empowerment starts with the individual whose actions have to be explained psychologically, a study of self-empowerment cannot do without the expertise of psychology. And last but not least, self-empowerment is also about a finding that can be observed throughout society and affects social life and, in substance, mostly specific political issues. Therefore, the political science view of the subject matter must not be missing. These considerations explain the composition of the group of researchers who have come together on this issue and who are also the authors of this book.

We define societal self-empowerment as the conscious violation of legal and non-legal norms for political, idealistic and ethical reasons, this in particular in distinction to the field of classical crime. This definition is therefore quite broad and includes various forms of and motives for self-empowerment. In our analyses, we have identified two forms of self-empowerment: on the one hand, forms in which the violation of a legal or non-legal rule primarily serves to draw attention to an issue. The norm itself is not questioned, but its general validity is ultimately confirmed (for example in the case of a school strike). We call this form of self-empowerment instrumental self-empowerment. It refers to the concept of civil disobedience, which derives its effectiveness precisely from the violation of the rule. However, the definition is also open to forms of self-empowerment in which the violation of the norm should primarily act as such, as an expression of distance and rejection, be it of a certain political decision, the rule violated, but not least also of the political system as a whole, which has produced this rule. We consider this type of self-empowerment, which we see as potentially problematic for coexistence in the community, to be expressive self-empowerment. We find clear empirical indications that expressive self-empowerment is an expression of the perception of the affected people that their political positions are not or not sufficiently represented in the political system.

Based on this definition and delimitation of the topic, the investigation is divided into various sections, which are reflected in the chapters of the book. It begins with the exact structuring of the subject, above all from a legal perspective. How does the legal system deal with different forms of self-empowerment by society? How far do legal justification grounds, fundamental rights or also state-philosophical considerations extend? How does the legal system react to the observed violations of non-legal conventions? Do they represent a welcome impulse for a political-democratic development and renewal, or should the legal system oppose them—by means of new legal delimitations?

Following this, we take the empirical view. In order to answer the question of how much self-empowerment currently exists, we have carried out two representative surveys at different times in order to specifically determine how the phenomenon of self-empowerment is reflected in numbers and contexts. On the one hand, we have abstractly asked when the respondents feel that they (do not) have to comply with rules. Is it permissible to follow one's conscience on occasion or does one always have to comply with rules? Is it even permissible to take the law into one's own hands? Or do you only have to comply with rules if you are at risk of being caught or if you agree with the rule? On the other hand, we have focused on two different empirical forms of self-empowerment and asked corresponding questions, on the one hand on the Fridays for Future demonstrations, on the other hand on Corona demonstrations. This content-related linking on the one hand and the repetition of the survey on the other hand have led to very informative results, which we first present in summary form.

Against the background of this empirical exploration, we consider—in two further chapters—the profiles of the Fridays for Future self-empowered and the Corona self-empowered persons. The empirical investigation of both aspects is carried out as parallel as possible in order to be able to draw comparisons between the two groups. This shows surprising differences between people who support Fridays for Future and those who are skeptical of the Corona measures. The former are typically well integrated into the political system, politically interested, they trust science and social media, but also believe that politicians try to keep their election promises. Supporters of the climate school strikes are satisfied with the problem-solving ability of the political system—with the central exception of climate protection -, they tend to parties to the left of the center, have high social trust and we find no evidence of alienation from the political system: Neither in terms of political self-efficacy nor in terms of dissatisfaction with democracy or the choice of protest or anti-system parties can deviations from the average of the respondents be seen.

This is not the case, however, with people who arrogate power to themselves with regard to the Corona rules. Their relationship to society and politics can be summarized with the keyword alienation: That these people are dissatisfied with Corona policy and consider the corresponding restrictions to be unjustified is self-evident. What is more striking is the low interpersonal trust of these people, which is also accompanied by significantly lower trust in democracy and the rule of law as well as lower satisfaction with democracy than the average. The significantly higher inclination to abstention and to voting for the AfD also points in this direction, as does the mistrust of science and public media, the trust in social media and the pronounced conspiracy mentality.

In a subsequent discussion chapter, we then sum up, so to speak, and discuss further conclusions from the results. In particular, we examine from a sociological and psychological perspective the thesis that expressive self-empowerment reflects a representational gap. In the past fifteen years, many highly consequential decisions have been made—from the rescue of the euro to migration policy to the fight against the Corona pandemic with the help of far-reaching restrictions on basic rights—which also received outstanding public attention. Nevertheless, the established parties in the Bundestag were largely in agreement with each other, often there were hardly any significantly divergent positions if one leaves out the details. This, it seems, could have led to a lot of frustration among supporters of the non-represented position, which was reflected politically in alienation from the representative democracy, which then led to expressive self-empowerment.

A final conclusion serves to assess and look to the future. The big question is how, in particular, the potentially harmful expressive self-empowerment can be countered, how the perceived representational gap can be closed and how the necessary trust in the community, in particular in the performance capability of our political system, can be maintained or restored. Only if we trust and—rightly—can trust, will we be able to master the current crises and also cope with future crises that will come.

What is Societal Self-Empowerment? 2

Societal self-empowerment is a phenomenon that relates to rules and rule violations. Rules and rule violations are a central subject of legal studies. For this reason, it makes sense to approach societal self-empowerment from a legal perspective and to measure it legally, thus structuring, classifying and making it understandable.

2.1 Self-Empowerment as an Idealistic, Political or also Ethically Motivated Violation of Law

Empowerment is the conferral of power, from a legal point of view the conferral of legal power, the entitlement or also the provision with a right. In this sense, a legal empowerment is only needed by the state according to the concept of the modern constitutional state. The state is correspondingly entrusted with tasks, equipped with competences and powers (Straßburger in print). In contrast, man is of course free. He acts—for which John Locke stands in particular in the context of state philosophy (Locke 1992 [1689]: 2. Abhandlung, Kap. 5)—on the basis of pre-existing freedom rights, which can be opposed to state power. Unlike the state, man therefore does not need legal empowerment at first.

However, the freedom of the one must be brought into line with the freedom of the other. For this purpose, the state is empowered by society and equipped with competences to reconcile the individual spheres of freedom, first and foremost to safeguard social peace and security. On the basis of this empowerment, the state creates a legal order. This legalizes the natural freedoms of man and at the same time restricts them in order to take into account the freedoms of all others. The freedom of the individual in turn becomes an entitlement, in this sense therefore a legal empowerment, which has a certain scope and certain limits.

P. Kirsch et al., *Societal Self-empowerment in Germany*, https://doi.org/10.1007/978-3-658-40865-7_2

Within the legal system, a further distinction is then made (Siegel 2022: Rdnr. 396 ff.). For example, there are legal entitlements that are based directly on the naturally underlying and constitutionally guaranteed freedoms, such as the right to build on one's own property anchored in building law (freedom to build), or the commercial right to operate a business (freedom to pursue a trade). Administrative regulatory regimes are basically preventive in nature in these areas, so they are intended to enable and restrict the exercise of the relevant freedoms as little as possible. Approval decisions are therefore typically not at the discretion of the authority, but are to be made positively if the factual requirements are met (bound decision). In contrast, however, there are also legal entitlements that are—without any constitutional basis—only conferred by the state, typically at the discretion of the authority and sometimes with repressive target orientation, as in German law, for example the right to use groundwater.

However, this internal differentiation is not relevant for the conceptual determination of societal self-empowerment. Because regardless of this differentiation, self-empowerment can be described as behaviour by which the actor consciously sets himself above the framework of the legally designed freedom, that is, above the limits of the individual entitlement. Self-empowerment is therefore the calculated violation of law or rules that is aimed at acquiring factual, non-legal, and therefore illegal power of action.

The aforementioned, provisional definition of self-empowerment is very broad. It includes classical crime as well as all other cases in which the individual is solely concerned with obtaining illegal, in particular material, advantages. What is characteristic of individual or societal self-empowerment, which is of interest here, is that it is based on idealistic, political or ethical motives at its core. Think of the school-law-breaking climate strike during school lessons or of the unauthorised demonstration by opponents of state measures to combat Covid-19. Societal self-empowerment is therefore to be defined in the present context as idealistic, political or ethically motivated violation of law.

2.2   Legal Justification of *Prima Facie* Self-Empowerments

The focus on such motivated violations of law now requires us to take a second legal level into account, on which the special motives for offenses play a role. On the second level, the level of justification, *prima facie* self-empowerments can be justified because of the underlying motives, that is, re-integrated into the legal system. This requires us to analyze the scope of the legal justification grounds in view of our object of investigation.

Justification grounds are contained to some extent in parliamentary statutory law. Ideal-typical examples of justification grounds in civil law are self-defense, emergency and self-help (§§ 227, 228, 229, 859 and 860 BGB). In criminal law, there are, for example, the criminal self-defense, the justifying emergency and the preliminary private arrest (§§ 32 and 34 StGB, § 127 Abs. 1 StPO). Administrative law also knows justification grounds; for example, if a conflict between private individuals is to be assessed in police law, justification grounds are to be taken into account which legitimate the action of one person towards the other person.

In all of the aforementioned areas of law, the justification of a factual self-empowerment exceeding the given legal authority usually requires that in the concrete, acute situation a predominantly significant legal good is threatened to be violated and that the self-empowerment serves to protect this legal good. Furthermore, there is usually no way to obtain state aid in time. The consequence of the relevant justification is the exception granted to the individual to defend the object of law in question himself. The state monopoly of exercising power thus recedes point-wise where the state power is unable to effectively protect the law. Instead, the individual is empowered to enforce the law in the concrete case. So the attacked may defend himself against the attacker, the owner may evict the intruder from the property and the robbed may arrest the caught thief until the police are on site.

Protection goods of the justification grounds for self-empowerments in civil law, criminal law and administrative law are always only concrete, tangible individual rights such as life, physical integrity, property and possession. Idealistic, political or even ethical positions are, however, not suitable as such from the outset to consider self-empowerments in accordance with the justification grounds of civil law, criminal law or administrative law as justified. The justification grounds do not take such positions into account.

In addition, on the level of constitutional law, fundamental rights, i.e. fundamental freedom and equality claims based on fundamental rights, can act as legitimizing action. On the one hand, the fundamental rights require a freedom- and equality-based design of statutory law. On the other hand, the fundamental rights radiate on the initially freedom-restricting statutory law that has to be interpreted and applied in accordance with the Constitution. A concrete example of the effect of the fundamental rights is the conscientious objection to military service, which is expressly guaranteed by fundamental rights in Art. 4 para. 3 sentence 2 GG. The statutory law, which provides for conscription (on the basis of Art.

12a para. 1 GG), provides for corresponding exceptions which take into account the fundamental right to refuse (see in particular the Act on the Refusal of Military Service on Conscientious Grounds of 09.08.2003, BGBl. I 2003, p. 1593, last amended by Act of 28.04.2011, BGBl. I 2011, p. 687). The second case, the radiation of fundamental rights on the existing, freedom-restricting statutory law, is illustrated by the school law dealing with the fact that Muslim parents forbid their daughter to participate in co-educational swimming lessons, which are however provided for by school law. The parents and their children can rely on the freedom of religion according to Art. 4 para. 1 GG in order to interpret and apply the state law (see for example a decision of the Federal Administrative Court from the year 2013, BVerwGE 147, 362: "The individual pupil can, based on religious conduct guidelines which he regards as decisive, only in exceptional cases demand exemption from a lesson."). In practice, mediation solutions are sought and found which, on the one hand, take into account the state school mission (Art. 7 para. 1 GG), on the other hand the freedom of religion of the parents and children.

Thus, fundamental rights positions can lead to the result that *prima facie* existing self-empowerments are re-integrated into the law. Unlike in the case of the legal justification grounds of civil law, criminal law and administrative law, not only concrete, individual protective interests such as physical integrity or property can be invoked with fundamental rights, but also more abstract and at the same time more far-reaching freedoms such as freedom of conscience, freedom of opinion and freedom of assembly. These freedoms can carry out idealistic, political and ethical motivated action. However, it should also be taken into account that the fundamental freedoms are in need of oncretisation in many parts and are above all also subject to restrictions. The regulating, democratically legitimate legislator and the administrative authorities applying the law have considerable decision-making powers in this respect, which substantially relativize the importance of fundamental rights as a means of re-integrating *prima facie*-self-empowerments into the law.

The most dramatic form of legitimation of self-empowerment anchored in the Basic Law can be found in the provision of Article 20(4) GG, which was inserted into the Basic Law as part of the emergency legislation in 1968. This is the right of resistance, which has been known and controversially discussed in state philosophy for centuries. Article 20(4) GG reads: "All Germans shall have the right of resistance against anyone who undertakes to eliminate this order, if other remedies are not possible." (The term "order" refers to the liberal-democratic constitutional order.) The right of resistance applies to the state authority as well as to private forces that attempt to eliminate the constitutional order. It allows all necessary acts of resistance that are aimed at preserving this order. Again, it is assumed that state aid cannot be obtained. The right of resistance thus intervenes in a situation in which the legal order of the community is wobbling. The Basic Law attests to the legality of the actions of anyone who resists in order to preserve this order. The private, initially rule-breaking application of force is thus legitimized on a constitutional level and thus re-integrated into the law.

The idealistic, political or ethical violation of the law, the subject of our investigation, differs in its target direction, of course, from the type of violation of the law that is legitimized by the right of resistance. The societal self-empowerment does not aim to defend itself from a threat to the constitutional order in order to protect and assert it, but rather it aims at addressing actual or alleged deficiencies within the existing and intact order. The conditions of Article 20(4) of the Basic Law are thus clearly not met in acts of societal self-empowerment.

Finally, no explicit normative basis has a legitimizing legal idea, which goes back to the Heidelberg legal philosopher and former Minister of Justice in the Weimar Republic Gustav Radbruch. Initially a convinced legal positivist, Radbruch formulated in 1946 under the immediate impression of National Socialism, "that the positive law, secured by statute and power has priority even if it is substantively unjust and impractical, unless the contradiction of the positive law to justice reaches such an intolerable degree that the law as 'wrong law' has to give way to justice." (Radbruch 1946: 107) Even this, later so-called Radbruch formula therefore aims to justify *prima facie* existing violations of the law and thus to attribute them to the law, here understood as justice in the material sense. The criterion is the unacceptability of the application of the law or loyalty to the law. Unlike the right of resistance, which is based on external circumstances, namely the serious endangerment of the constitutional order, in the Radbruch formula the unacceptability of compliance with the law is in the factual situation, that is, an internal, moral and conscience-related circumstance.

The Radbruch formula has actually been used in judicial practice—in a few individual cases—for the one hand in the processing of individual consequences of National Socialism (for example BGHZ 3, 94 (107); BVerfGE 23, 98), on the other hand for the coping with the inner-German wall guards problem (BVerfGE 95, 96). For the legal classification of current phenomena of societal self-empowerment, the Radbruch formula plays just as little a role as the constitutional right of resistance.

The concept of civil disobedience, on the other hand, which can be relevant in cases of societal self-empowerment, has no legally justifying effect. Civil disobedience is generally defined as a form of political participation through conscious, attention-generating violation of the law. This violation of the law is not legally justified. It is precisely the essential element of civil disobedience to point out certain deficiencies by means of the intended violation of a norm, that is, the illegality of a behaviour, in order to bring a political concern to light. As with the right of resistance, legal rules are broken in civil disobedience. However, unlike the right of resistance, the aim of civil disobedience is not to take action against a threat to the constitutional order and to stabilise it by breaking the law, but to work within the existing and stable constitutional order to achieve certain political objectives or to eliminate perceived deficiencies. Not a general duty of civil obedience, which does not exist, but specific individual norms such as § 123 StGB (trespass), § 185 StGB (insult), § 223 StGB (bodily injury), § 240 StGB (coercion) or § 303 StGB (damage of property) are violated. The persons concerned do not reject these specific norms as such, but rather confirm their validity. Because the persons concerned assume that the attention for the concern follows precisely from the fact that a norm accepted as valid is violated. In a certain way, civil disobedience thus acts, regardless of the political concern in each case, to confirm the legal order. The legal order is instrumentalised to bring a certain issue to the fore.

Against this background, the category of civil disobedience fits for numerous cases of societal self-empowerment. If pupils organise a climate strike during school time, they want to emphasise the importance of their concern by violating the school law. If citizens demonstrate against government measures to combat Covid-19 in contradiction to the limits of the right of assembly, they accept the violation of norms or even make use of the media attention that results from the violation of norms for their own purposes. And even verbal or physical attacks on local politicians are not due to personal enmity, but to political motives—which does not change the reprehensible nature of such attacks.

In summary, it can be said that violations of the law motivated by idealism, politics or ethics cannot be justified legally in most cases. The justification grounds of civil law, criminal law and administrative law are based exclusively on concrete and concretely endangered individual rights such as life, physical integrity, property and possession. In turn, fundamental rights positions can only be used to a very limited extent to legitimize *prima facie* apparent legal violations in the context of societal self-empowerment. The fundamental rights protect, inter alia, the right to freedom of conscience, freedom of expression and freedom of assembly. However, the freedom protected by the Basic Law is subject to a considerable need for agreement and thus concretisation, which is why the Basic Law leaves corresponding leeway for the democratically legitimate legislature and the administrative authority applying the law. This in turn reduces the scope for justifying violations of the norms that fill these leeways. The constitutional right of resistance only comes into consideration in the event of a serious threat to the constitutional order as a whole. And Radbruch's formula serves to deal with dictatorships. Against this background, it is understandable that actions within the framework of societal self-empowerment fall to some extent into the—legally not justifying—category of civil disobedience.

2.3 Two Examples of Rights-Infringing Self-Empowerment

The classification of societal self-empowerment can be illustrated using two examples.

Fridays for Future demonstrations during school time violate—here exemplarily for Baden-Württemberg—the school attendance obligation regulated in §§ 73 ff. of the Baden-Württemberg School Act. The clear regulations do not allow exceptions directly in favor of the demonstrating students or dispensation possibilities of the school. An interpretation that places the fundamental right to freedom of expression and assembly of the students (Art. 5 para. 1 sentence 1 and Art. 8 para. 1 GG) in the foreground is not possible in view of the clear wording of the regulations. However, the provisions of §§ 73 ff. SchulG BW are not unconstitutional. They concretize the school task of the state anchored in the constitutional rank (Art. 7 para. 1 GG). When the constitutional positions are compared, it can be assumed that a design of the school lesson, which does not allow demonstration participation during school time—with whatever content-related concern—does not violate the fundamental rights of the students. The legal justification grounds of civil law, criminal law and administrative law are just as little relevant as the constitutional right of resistance or even Radbruch's formula.

This shows that a legal justification for the Fridays for Future demonstrations as an expression of societal self-empowerment is conceivable from the outset only in accordance with the basic rights of the actors. However, the basic rights justification also fails. The actions of the pupils thus constitute a form of civil disobedience.

A second example: In Baden-Württemberg, the obligation to wear a mouth-nose protection in certain situations to combat the Covid-19 pandemic results from § 3 para. 1 of the Corona Ordinance of Baden-Württemberg, which is based on a legal basis in § 32 of the Infection Protection Act of the Federal Republic of Germany. The refusal to wear a mouth-nose protection violates this obligation and can result in a fine. The obligation interferes with the general freedom of action protected by Art. 2 para. 1 GG, possibly also with the freedom of expression (Art. 5 para. 1 sentence 1 GG). It also applies here that restrictions on the freedom of the persons concerned can be justified by a sufficiently important public interest and in compliance with the principle of proportionality. In this case, the freedom rights of the persons concerned stand in opposition to the aim pursued by the mask obligation, which in turn has constitutional rank. According to Art. 2 para. 2 sentence 1 GG, the state is even obliged to take active protective action to protect life and health (constitutional duty of protection). Depending on the individual case, the freedom of action of the persons concerned on the one hand and the purpose pursued by the mask obligation, the protection of life and health of the people, on the other hand, have to be reconciled. If one assumes that the coordination between the interests concerned has been successful as a whole, § 3 para. 1 of the CoronaVO BW is also constitutional and violations of the ordinance remain illegal from a constitutional perspective. Other possible justification grounds do not come into consideration in this context.

To the extent that violations of the obligation to wear a mouth-nose protection can appear to be an expression of societal self-empowerment, it thus becomes clear that also this form of societal self-empowerment can be legally justified only to the extent of the basic rights, but that also here the legal justification—subject to individual cases of a possibly failed fundamental rights balancing—fails. Also this manifestation of societal self-empowerment remains illegal. Whether it can thus be classified as a form of civil disobedience is, however, somewhat more problematic than in the case of the Fridays for Future demonstrations. Because here the violation of the law does not necessarily serve to draw attention to a political issue. Ultimately, it depends on the assessment of the individual case.

2.4   Self-Empowerment within the Law

In addition to the socially self-empowering violation of law, there are cases of societal self-empowerment that take place entirely within the law, that is, they occur from the outset without any violation of law. Self-empowerment in this variant is characterized by the violation of not legal, but exclusively social norms and conventions. Examples are the brutalization of democratic discourse, the spread of "alternative facts" to justify one's own positions and the establishment of—still maintaining the state monopoly of force—citizen militias to ensure security.

Self-empowerment within the law reflects a variety of developments within society. Constitutionally, it is a form of exercising private and political freedom. Self-empowerment within the law can often point to existing deficiencies and problems and set impulses for improving social coexistence. The violation of established social norms and conventions gives the decisive impetus for appropriate political changes. Sometimes, however, manifestations of self-empowerment within the law can also be harmful. In this—and only in this—case, the reaction required by the constitutionally guided politics should be to legally prohibit the actions. Recent examples of parliamentary reactions to harmful forms of self-empowerment within the law were, for example, the Act to Strengthen the Protection of Enforcement Officers and Rescue Workers of 2017 and the Act to Combat Right-Wing Extremism and Hate Crime of 2020.

From a constitutional perspective, the issue of societal self-empowerment within the law refers to the concept of the constitutional prerequisite or also the constitutional expectation (Isensee 2011). Legally granted and guaranteed freedom only becomes real if the holders of fundamental rights accept their freedom (Kirchhof 1998: 61) and exercise it in accordance with the freedom of all others. As a liberal state, the constitutional state—in other words—is dependent on conditions that it cannot guarantee without losing its liberalism (Böckenförde 1991: 112 f.). The state must trust the freedom and democracy of the people in this respect.

References

Böckenförde, Ernst-Wolfgang. 1991. Die Entstehung des Staates als Vorgang der Säkularisation, in: Ernst-Wolfgang Böckenförde: *Recht, Staat, Freiheit*, Frankfurt: Suhrkamp, 92–114.
Isensee, Josef. [3]2011. Grundrechtsvoraussetzungen und Verfassungserwartungen an die Grundrechtsausübung, in: Josef Isensee and Paul Kirchhof (eds.): *Handbuch des Staatsrechts der Bundesrepublik Deutschland, Bd. IX*. Heidelberg: C.F. Müller, 264–411.
Kirchhof, Paul. 1998. Die Einheit des Staates in seinen Verfassungsvoraussetzungen, in: Otto Depenheuer, Markus Heintzen und Matthias Jestaedt (eds.): *Die Einheit des Staates*. Heidelberg: C.F. Müller, 51–69.
Locke, John. 1992 [1689]. *Zwei Abhandlungen über die Regierung*. Frankfurt: Suhrkamp.
Radbruch, Gustav. 1946. Gesetzliches Unrecht und übergesetzliches Recht. *Süddeutsche Juristenzeitung* 1(5): 105–108.
Siegel, Thorsten. [14]2022. *Allgemeines Verwaltungsrecht*. Heidelberg: C.F. Müller.
Straßburger, Benjamin. in print. *Herrschaft als Auftrag. Der Verfassungsbegriff des demokratischen Konstitutionalismus und seine Bedeutung für die supranationale Integration Deutschlands*. Tübingen: Mohr Siebeck.

How Much Societal Self-Empowerment is There?

3

We have surveyed the extent of societal self-empowerment in Germany through two representative online surveys conducted primarily in July and December 2020 (see details in the appendix). In doing so, we have tried to get to the bottom of the extent of societal self-empowerment in two ways. On the one hand, we have asked our respondents to answer abstract questions about whether one always has to obey the law or whether there are exceptions, whether one is allowed to take the law into one's own hands or whether one is only obliged to obey the law under certain conditions. On the other hand, specific questions about individual behaviour in particularly prominent and much-discussed current cases of self-empowerment were to be answered, namely with regard to the school climate strikes of the Fridays for Future (FFF) movement and the compliance with Corona rules. In the following, we will first present the results of our survey for the abstract questions and then for the concrete societal self-empowerment in the cases of Fridays for Future and Corona.

3.1 The Abstract Level

On the abstract level of general ideas about how important respondents consider it to obey the law, we asked three questions. The first question was: "In general, would you say that people should obey the law without exception, or are there exceptional occasions on which people should follow their consciences even if it means breaking the law?" Asking in this way—which emphasizes the exceptional character of breaking the law in a conflict of conscience—a broad majority of almost two thirds of our respondents (63.7%) take the view that one should be allowed to follow one's conscience in exceptional situations (Fig. 3.1). Only

P. Kirsch et al., *Societal Self-empowerment in Germany*, https://doi.org/10.1007/978-3-658-40865-7_3

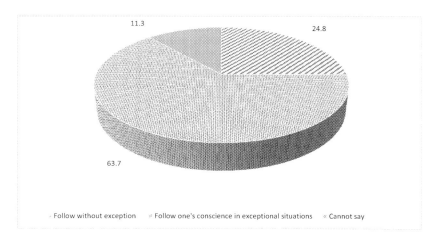

Fig. 3.1 Response proportions: "Must laws be followed without exception?" (Source: Own survey, own analysis)

around a quarter of respondents (24.8%) say that one must always obey the law.
[1]

Since this question has also been asked five times in Germany as part of the Role of Government Survey of the International Social Survey Programme (ISSP) between 1985 and 2016, a corresponding historical comparison is possible at this point (cf. Table 3.1). Our value for those who think that one must always obey the law is approximately at the long-term average (25.2%),[2] well below the value of the last survey in 2016, when just under 35% of those surveyed said that one must always follow the law. Conversely, 52.5% of those surveyed in 2016 as part of the ISSP survey said they would follow their conscience in exceptional cases, while the average over all surveys was 63.7%, and thus again close to the value we found. Whether these changes since 2016 reflect a greater willingness to self-empower, which could be caused, for example, by current events such as

[1] The differences between our two surveys are minimal on this question: In the first survey, 64% were of the opinion that one should be allowed to follow one's conscience in exceptional situations, 25% said that one must always obey the law and 10.7% could not make up their minds. In the second survey, the corresponding values were 63.2%, 24.6% and 12.1%.

[2] In 1990 and 1996, separate surveys were conducted in East and West Germany. These were taken into account as separate surveys in the calculation of the mean. However, the two parts of the country differed only marginally on this issue.

Table 3.1 Agreement (in percent) to the unconditional observance of laws according to data from the Role-of-Government survey, 1985–2016

	Laws must be followed without exception	Follow conscience in exceptional cases	Undecided/No answer
1985	11.5	85.0	3.5
1990 (West)	23.2	68.3	8.5
1990 (East)	24.6	65.0	10.4
1996 (West)	23.1	61.1	15.9
1996 (East)	24.7	60.1	15.2
2006	34.1	53.5	12.4
2016	34.9	52.6	12.6
Average	25.2	63.7	11.2

(Source: ISSP 1985, 1990, 1996, 2006, 2016)

the Fridays for Future protests or the dissatisfaction of certain population groups with the Corona restrictions, is not implausible, but requires further investigation.

While the majority of those surveyed appear to be willing to follow their conscience in exceptional situations, even if the behavior contradict the law, a general acceptance of societal self-empowerment cannot be claimed by any means. So, only a minority of less than one fifth (18.1%) of our respondents think it is right that people take the law into their own hands, while almost two thirds (63.5%) of respondents reject such behavior (Fig. 3.2).[3] The very different responses to these two questions suggest that societal self-empowerment is apparently acceptable as an exception under very special circumstances—as the first question suggests—for many respondents, but that a large majority rejects a general disregard for social and state rules, as implied by the second question, which much more generally inquires if people would take the law into their own hands.

While respondents in the previously discussed questions had to choose one option each (either follow laws without exception or follow conscience in exceptional cases, etc.), at a later point in the first (but not the second) survey, we asked about various options for self-empowering behavior separately (Fig. 3.3). In line with the results presented above, the majority of respondents also said in a separate question that one must follow one's conscience in exceptional situations

---

[3] Again, the differences between the two surveys are marginal. In the first (second) survey, 18.3% (17.8%) thought that one could take the law into one's own hands; 62.9% (64.1%) did not find this, 18.6% (17.7%) were undecided.

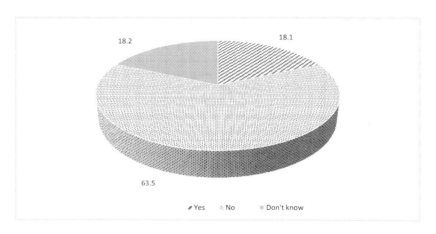

Fig. 3.2 Answer shares: "Can one take the law into one's own hands?" (Source: Own survey, own evaluation)

(59.7%), while significantly fewer respondents (33.8%) said that one must always follow the law.

Although most respondents actually perceive these two options as opposites, as shown by a highly significant negative correlation between the two items (r = −0.673, p = 0.000), it is striking that the proportion of respondents who generally agree that one must always adhere to the law is higher when the two statements (adhere to the law vs. follow conscience) are asked separately (33.8 vs. 25%). This could support the interpretation that, for some respondents, the option of violating the law for conscience' sake is only acceptable as a rare exception.

The data from Fig. 3.3 is also interesting in that other reasons for violating the law find little support. Only 12.5% of respondents make compliance with the law dependent on the government's compliance with the law, and the idea that one must only comply with the law if one agrees with it or that non-compliance has negative consequences (e.g. punishment) is only minimally accepted (2.7% and 3%).

In view of the results of the abstract questions on societal self-empowerment, it can be concluded from the survey that self-empowerment is by no means generally accepted by society. Rather, most of those surveyed demand compliance with the law from themselves and their fellow citizens. Deviations are only accepted to a limited extent, namely in the context of conscience conflicts. The next step

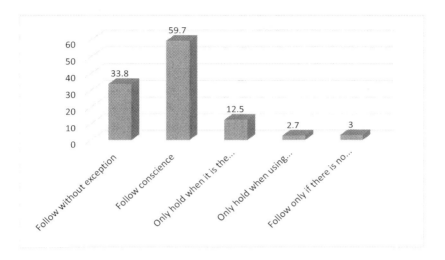

Fig. 3.3 Proportion of responses for self-empowerment, separate question. (Source: Own survey, own evaluation)

is now to ask whether this finding changes if we go one step down the ladder of abstraction and confront our respondents with concrete cases of possible societal self-empowerment. We present the results of the assessment of the Fridays for Future movement and the compliance with the coronavirus rules by our respondents in the next two sections.

3.2 Societal Self-Empowerment and the Fridays for Future Movement

The Fridays for Future (FFF) movement, originally founded by Swedish high-school student Greta Thunberg in August 2018, serves as our first concrete case with which we want to measure the extent of societal self-empowerment in Germany. The goal of the FFF movement is to enact climate protection measures that go beyond the measures adopted so far and promise to achieve the goal of the 2015 Paris UN Climate Conference to limit global warming to 1.5°C above the pre-industrial era. This movement has received considerable public attention in Germany in 2019 and even influenced the political agenda (Raisch and Zohlnhöfer 2020).

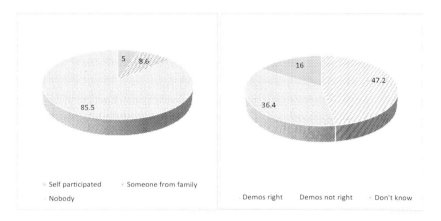

Fig. 3.4 Participation in FFF demonstrations (left, Fig. 3.4a) and assessment of the FFF demonstrations as right (right, Fig. 3.4b). (Source: Own survey, own evaluation)

We can speak of societal self-empowerment with regard to the FFF movement because the central instrument of the movement is demonstrations that take place every Friday during school time (so-called climate strikes). This usually contradicts the school obligation of the pupils, so that we can speak of societal self-empowerment.

Our survey included three questions dealing with the climate school strikes. First, it was about whether the respondent him/herself or another family member [4] participated in the demonstrations (Fig. 3.4a). While around five percent of the respondents in both surveys said they had participated in FFF demonstrations themselves, another 8.6% said that family members (probably often the children) had been involved in such activities. Broader than the participation in FFF activities was the sympathy of the respondents for the movement. Just under half of the respondents (47.2%) found the demonstrations right, a good third (36.4%) rejected them (Fig. 3.4b).

For our purposes, it is of course central that the participants in the demonstrations have violated the compulsory school attendance. If we explicitly ask respondents whether they think the demonstrations should take place during

---

[4] Since the majority of the FFF participants are likely to have been minors, but only people over the age of 17 were surveyed in our survey, we tried to better assess the extent of unauthorized behavior with the question of the participation of family members in the school strikes.

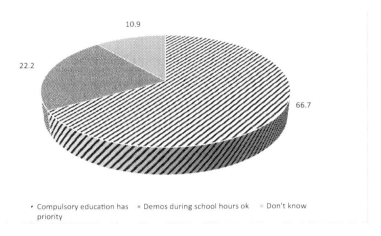

Fig. 3.5 Response proportions: Priority for compulsory education or not? (Source: Own survey, Own analysis)

school time or whether the compulsory school attendance should take precedence, the support for the school strikes decreases. Only between a quarter and a fifth of the respondents (22.2%) think that the demonstrations should take place during school time, while two thirds (66.7%) think that the compulsory school attendance should take precedence (Fig. 3.5).[5]

If one wants to map societal self-empowerment with respect to the Fridays for Future movement in an aggregated way, it makes sense to combine the three items mentioned. For each question, we coded the answer option with 1 that expresses support for the FFF school strikes (school strikes correct, own participation, participation of family member, support for demonstrations during school time), while all other answer options were coded with 0. Subsequently, the three

---

[5] The numbers from both surveys are relatively similar: In the first (second) survey, 5.0% (5.1%) of the respondents said that they had participated themselves, 10.1% (6.8%) reported that a relative had participated and 83.9% (87.4%) said that no family member had participated in an FFF demonstration. In the first (second) survey, 48.3% (45.8%) of the respondents supported the demonstrations, 35.1% (37.9%) considered them to be wrong, 16.3% (15.6%) could not decide. Finally, 23.8% (20.2%) of the respondents in the first (second) survey found it correct that the demonstrations took place during school time, while 64.5% (69.5%) gave precedence to the compulsory school attendance. 11.5% (10.0%) were undecided.

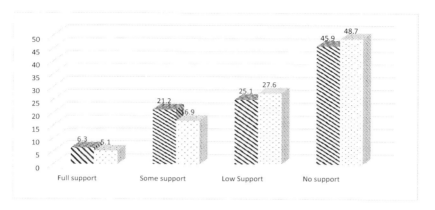

Fig. 3.6 Aggregation of items for Fridays for Future. (Source: Own survey, own evaluation. Hatched bars: Survey July 2020, dotted bars: Survey December 2020)

recoded items were added up. For example, respondents who not only gave priority to the school obligation over the demonstrations, but also neither participated themselves nor had a family member who participated, and finally also considered the demonstrations to be wrong, were assigned the value 0 ("no support"). Respondents who only supported the FFF movement in one or two items received the corresponding intermediate values.

Figure 3.6 shows the result of this aggregation for both surveys separately. Across both surveys, just under half of the respondents (47.1%) did not express any clear support for the climate strike movement at any point, while on the other hand only 5.8% supported all aspects of the FFF movement. Here too, therefore, there is a—perhaps surprisingly—limited degree of societal self-empowerment in Germany.

3.3   Societal Self-Empowerment with Respect to Corona Restrictions

Towards the end of 2019, a new respiratory illness first appeared in Wuhan (China), caused by a previously unknown coronavirus (SARS-CoV-2). The disease COVID-19, caused by the virus, quickly spread outside of China as well, and on March 11, 2020, the WHO declared the disease a global pandemic. In mid-March 2020, a number of far-reaching measures to limit the spread of the disease were adopted in the Federal Republic of Germany, including the widespread restriction of social contacts, the closure of schools, restaurants, many stores and service providers of body care, border closures, and the obligation to wear everyday masks, e.g. in shops and public transport.

Since March 2020, the politics of the coronavirus has been the dominant political topic in Germany. Since March 2020, the data of the Politbarometer of the Forschungsgruppe Wahlen (2022) have shown the pandemic to be the most important problem in Germany, e.g. in March 2021 85% of those surveyed named Corona as one of the two most important problems in Germany. This topic thus dominated the political agenda of the time since March 2020.

From the perspective of societal self-empowerment, the acceptance of the measures to contain the pandemic (hereafter referred to as Corona measures) is particularly interesting. On the one hand, the measures were obviously associated with the restriction of a large number of basic rights, so that they interfered massively with individual lifestyle. In this respect, the incentives could have been particularly great not to comply with the rules. On the other hand, it was particularly important that the population complied with these rules in order to successfully contain the spread of COVID-19.

We have measured the willingness to self-empower in relation to the Corona measures by four items. First, the respondents were asked whether they had complied with the restrictions (similar to van Rooij et al. 2020), then it was asked more specifically whether the respondents had already downloaded the Corona Warning App, which had been made available shortly before the first survey, or whether they intended to do so, whether they would be willing to be vaccinated if a vaccine were available, and whether they had participated in demonstrations against the restrictions imposed by the Corona measures.

It should be noted in this context that only the first question reflects societal self-empowerment in the strict sense, because only then is it about complying with binding rules, while neither the use of the Corona warning app nor the vaccination were legally required (vaccines were not even available when both surveys were conducted). However, our understanding of societal self-empowerment goes beyond the violation of laws and, in the case of the warning app and vaccination, there can be no doubt that these were two very central components of the Corona strategy of the political decision-makers in Germany. Accordingly, the refusal to participate (even if this refusal is legal) is quite relevant to the question of the extent of societal self-empowerment. Similarly, participation in demonstrations cannot be classified as societal self-empowerment in the strict sense if they are approved and corresponding rules are observed—on the contrary, the right to

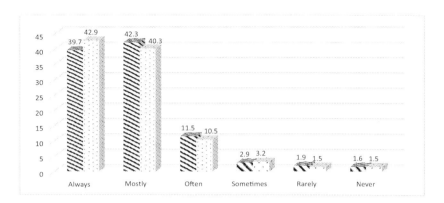

Fig. 3.7 Compliance with Corona rules (self-report). (Source: Own survey, own evaluation. Hatched bars: survey July 2020, dotted bars: survey December 2020 (first published in Kirsch et al. 2022: 51))

demonstrate is of course a fundamental democratic participation right. However, many of the demonstrations against the Corona restrictions were characterized precisely by the fact that certain rules (e.g. with regard to minimum distance and wearing masks) were deliberately not observed (Heinze and Weisskircher 2022: 2),[6] so that one can also speak of societal self-empowerment here.

However, how widespread was societal self-empowerment with regard to the Corona measures among our respondents? Most respondents in both surveys said that they had always (39.7 or 42.9%) or mostly (42.3 or 40.3%) complied with the Corona rules, while only very small minorities (3.5 or 3.0%) said that they had rarely or never complied with the rules (Fig. 3.7). It should be noted at this point that these are self-reports by the respondents, which cannot be objectively verified. Nevertheless, the picture shows a widespread compliance with rules by the respondents, although, as described, this involved far-reaching interventions in individual lifestyle.

This picture was also reflected in a relatively high level of satisfaction with the work of the federal government in containing the Corona pandemic in the summer of 2020: more than two thirds of our respondents (68.3%) were satisfied, 37% even were very satisfied. This satisfaction is likely due to the fact that, at

---

[6] Compare, for example, https://www.deutschlandfunk.de/covid-19-pandemie-corona-demonstrationen-positionen-und.2897.de.html?dram:article_id=476457 (last accessed on 28.10.2020).

the time of the survey, the number of cases had declined sharply as a result of the measures taken and increasingly liberalisations could be adopted. In contrast, the pandemic situation had changed considerably by the time of the second survey, with the number of new infections having increased massively. This change was also reflected to some extent in the assessment of the federal government's activities in combating the Corona crisis, with satisfaction in December 2020 only at 55% of respondents, and only 25% were very satisfied, compared to 37% in summer. However, it is noteworthy that, despite the declining satisfaction, compliance with the Corona rules remained at the high level of summer.

A more nuanced picture emerges when it comes to the willingness to install the Corona Warning App, which has been available since 16 June 2020 (and thus two weeks before the start of our first survey) (Fig. 3.8). Around a third (32.2%) of those surveyed in July 2020 said that they had already installed the app, while just under a tenth (9.5%) claimed that they could not install the app for technical reasons, e.g. because they do not own a mobile phone or because their mobile phone does not meet the technical minimum requirements for the app. In this group, the non-installation cannot be understood as self-empowerment. On the other hand, a strong minority of 45.3% of those surveyed said that it was rather or even very unlikely that they would download the app. In particular, the nearly one-third of those surveyed who considered it very unlikely to install the app could well be seen as a group that could have a tendency towards self-empowerment, as they refused to use a central instrument of the state's pandemic response.

Interestingly, five months later, these data had changed very little. Although the number of those who had installed the app had increased in the meantime and the number of those who said they were likely or very likely to install the app had decreased accordingly, the proportion of those who were rather or very unlikely to install the app had not decreased significantly.

The willingness to be vaccinated against Corona was also surprisingly low among our respondents, considering that only a vaccination of the majority of the population appeared to be a realistic perspective to return to normality. Nevertheless, in July 2020, only just under 55% of respondents said that they were very likely or quite likely to be vaccinated (Fig. 3.9). In contrast, the 13.8% of respondents who said that it was not at all likely that they would be vaccinated appear to be particularly unresponsive to calls for joint action against the pandemic. Hence, at least these people can be considered as self-empowered, even though it should be noted that, at the time of the survey, firstly, infection rates had fallen sharply everywhere and, secondly, no vaccine was available, so the question was hypothetical.

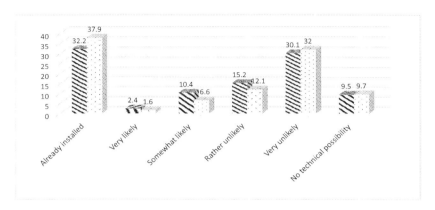

Fig. 3.8 Installation of the Corona warning app. (Source: Own survey, Own analysis. Hatched bars: July 2020 survey, dotted bars: December 2020 survey)

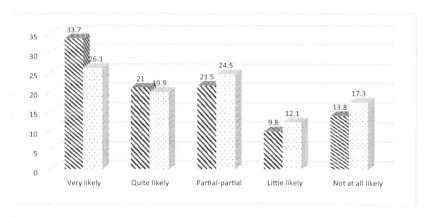

Fig. 3.9 Readiness for vaccination against Corona. (Source: Own survey, Own analysis. Hatched bars: July 2020 survey, dotted bars: December survey. 2020)

However, even under the impression of sharply increased infection rates and the more realistic perspective of a vaccine being available soon (application for approval of the first vaccine in the EU on 01 December 2020), the willingness to be vaccinated among the respondents of our second survey in December 2020 remained low, indeed it had even fallen compared to the first survey: Only 46%

of our respondents were now very likely or likely to be vaccinated, almost 30% considered it to be quite or very unlikely that they would be vaccinated.

Finally, we take a look at participation in demonstrations against the Corona restrictions (Fig. 3.10). It turns out that only a very small part of our respondents say that they have participated in such demonstrations, namely less than 4%. This does not seem to underestimate the participation in these demonstrations at least, because the number of participants in such demonstrations for the year 2020 is estimated to be a few tens of thousands in the literature (Grande et al. 2021: 5–6), although the mobilization potential could have been significantly higher (Grande et al. 2021).

Similar to the above self-empowerment in the case of the Fridays for Future movement, an aggregation of the different items should also be attempted for Corona compliance. Again, all variables are recoded so that higher values indicate a higher degree of self-empowerment. In addition, the additional variance is used that arises because the Corona variables (with the exception of the question on participation in demonstrations) were not dichotomous, but rather in several stages. For example, the general question of compliance with the Corona rules is coded 0 if answered with "Always kept to the rules", 1 for "mostly", 2 for "often", 3 for "sometimes", 4 for "rarely" and 5 for "never". A similar procedure is used for the other items, with the following responses being coded with

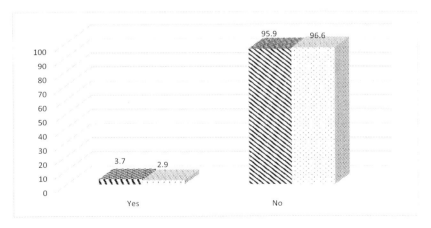

Fig. 3.10 Participation in demonstrations against Corona measures. (Source: Own survey, own evaluation. Hatched bars: survey July 2020, dotted bars: survey December 2020)

0 for the Corona warning app: The app has already been installed, is very likely to be installed and cannot be installed for technical reasons. Since there is only one dichotomous response option for the question of participation in demonstrations, non-participation is coded with 0 and participation with 2 (for details of the aggregation, see Appendix 1). Aggregating the four items, we obtain an index ranging from 0 (= always kept to the Corona restrictions, warning app installed, very likely vaccination, no participation in demonstrations) to 14 (never kept to the rules, installation of the app and vaccination very unlikely, participation in demonstrations against Corona restrictions). The corresponding distribution is shown in Fig. 3.11.

Even on this aggregated level, it becomes clear that the great majority of respondents comply with the rules (or at least claim to do so). Around half of the respondents (52 or 49 %) score 0 to 3 points on the 15-point scale. If one considers that respondents who mostly complied with the Corona restrictions, are likely to install the warning app, are quite likely to be vaccinated and have not participated in demonstrations, already have a value of 3, it becomes clear that these are extremely law-abiding people.

If one adds up all respondents up to a value of 5 (e.g. people who mostly adhered to the Corona restrictions, are likely to install the warning app, did not participate in demonstrations, but are unlikely to get vaccinated), just under three quarters of respondents (74.7 or 71.6%) can be classified as not susceptible to

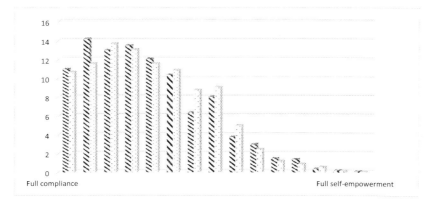

Fig. 3.11 Aggregation of items on Corona compliance (in percent of respondents). (Source: Own survey, own evaluation. Hatched bars: Survey July 2020, dotted bars: Survey December 2020)

societal self-empowerment—despite the massive restrictions described, which the measures to contain the Corona pandemic entailed. On the other hand, the proportion of hard societal self-empowerment with values of 10 and above (e.g. people who rarely adhered to the Corona restrictions, for whom it is rather unlikely that they will install the Corona warning app, who are unsure about vaccination and who participated in a demonstration against the Corona restrictions; value 10) is low at 3.7 or 3.0% of all respondents.

3.4 Societal Self-Empowerment in the Empirical Cases in Comparison

Finally, it has to be examined whether the persons who show themselves as self-empowered in the two empirical examples of our study, Fridays for Future and Corona, are the same groups of persons. In order to investigate this, we first formed a group of self-empowered persons in relation to the two empirical examples, which we set against a group of rule followers. For this purpose, we relied on the aggregated FFF and Corona scores introduced above. For Fridays for Future, we first defined those persons as self-empowered who showed support for FFF in at least one item (i.e. had a score between 1 and 3), and set this group against those respondents who had an aggregated value of 0, i.e. neither participated in FFF demonstrations nor found them right and also claimed priority of the duty to attend school. For the example of the Corona restrictions, we set the stricter criterion of an aggregated Corona compliance score between 0 and 3 for the rule followers, while respondents with an aggregated score of 4 and above were coded as Corona self-empowered.

The values set in bold in Table 3.2 show the relative proportions of four different groups: people who can be considered rule followers with regard to both FFF and Corona (cell 1), people who self-empower in one but not the other area (cells 2 and 3), and respondents who self-empower in both areas. If one assumes that there is only a certain group of people who, regardless of the subject, tend to self-empower, one would expect the majority of respondents to be in cells 1 (rule follower) and 4 (self-empowered). But this is not the case, as in these two cells there are significantly less than half of all respondents (together 43.1%). Rather, the numbers suggest that the majority of respondents are "selective self-empowered people", who largely follow the rules in certain areas, but are also willing to break the rules in others. Intriguingly, for our two empirical examples, there is even a tendency for respondents who can be considered self-empowered

Table 3.2 Self-empowerment at Fridays-for-Future and Corona

	No support for FFF	FFF supporter	Total
Corona rule follower	**20.4%**	**30.2%**	**50.6%**
	90.9% (strict)	*5.7% (strict)*	*96.6% (strict)*
	1	2	
Corona self-empowered	**26.7%**	**22.7%**	**49.4%**
	3.4% (strict)	*0.0% (strict)*	*3.4% (strict)*
	3	4	
Sum	**47.2%**	**52.8%**	
	94.3% (strict)	*5.7% (strict)*	

(Source: Own survey, own calculation)
*Note: The **wide** definition of self-empowerment is printed in bold and includes the proportion of people with aggregated Corona scores between 4 and 14, Corona rule followers have scores between 0 and 3. In FFF, people with an aggregated score of 1 to 3 are considered self-empowered under the broad definition, people with an aggregated score of 0 are considered rule followers. The **strict** definition of self-empowerment is set in italics and for the Corona measures includes the proportion of people with aggregated scores between 10 and 14, Corona rule followers have scores between 0 and 9. In FFF, people with an aggregated score of 3 are considered strict FFF supporters, all other people are not considered self-empowered.*

with regard to Corona to support FFF less and vice versa. So 57.2% of FFF supporters adhere to the Corona rules, while 54% of Corona self-empowered people give priority to school attendance, have not participated in the FFF demonstrations and consider them to be wrong.

However, these values are based on a very broad definition of societal self-empowerment. In a further step, we therefore empirically defined the concept more strictly: For the Fridays for Future questions, we now only consider those respondents as self-empowered who score the maximum value of 3, for the Corona questions we consider self-empowerment only from a value of 10 and more. The corresponding values can be found in Table 3.2 set in italics. Employing this much stricter definition, the number of self-empowered people naturally becomes much smaller and we therefore identify the majority of respondents (90.9%) as pure rule followers. However, what is more interesting is that we do not find a single person in both surveys taken together, that is, among more than 2,400 respondents, who is both a strict self-empowered person in the area of Fridays for Future and in the area of Corona measures.

Statistically, there is indeed a weak but highly significant negative correlation between self-empowerment in the areas of climate school strikes and Corona (measured by the respective aggregated index; rs $= -.159$, p $<.000$; $\tau = -.127$, p $<.000$).

3.5   Summary

What can be said about the extent of self-empowerment in Germany in 2020 from the data presented? First of all, we should highlight that the violation of rules is by no means a behaviour that is widely accepted in society. Only a minority think it is right when people take the law into their own hands, and we find hardly any approval for the idea that compliance with rules should be restricted to cases in which one agrees with the rule or in which one expects negative consequences. At most, in conflicts of conscience there is a greater willingness to accept rule-breaking. While a longitudinal view is only possible on the basis of a single question, the level of abstract self-empowerment in 2020 does not appear to be above the long-term average, although it is significantly higher than in 2016, the year of the last relevant survey.

When looking at specific cases of possible societal self-empowerment, the majority of respondents also show rather rule-compliant behaviour (at least according to their own statements). Nevertheless, we also find a significant number of people who sympathise with non-rule-compliant behaviour or even break rules in specific cases. However, it depends on the specific subject whether people are willing to self-empower or not. People who are willing to participate in climate strikes are therefore by no means necessarily less compliant with the Corona restrictions—on the contrary, the opposite seems to be the case.

References

Forschungsgruppe Wahlen. 2022. Wichtige Probleme in Deutschland. abrufbar unter https://www.forschungsgruppe.de/Umfragen/Politbarometer/Langzeitentwicklung_-_Themen_im_Ueberblick/Politik_II/9_Probleme_1_1.xlsx (last accessed 18.03.2022).

Grande, Edgar, Swen Hutter, Sophia Hunger, and Eylem Kanol. 2021. *Alles Covidioten? Politische Potenziale des Corona-Protests in Deutschland.* Wissenschaftszentrum Berlin für Sozialforschung: Discussion Paper ZZ 2021–601, available at https://bibliothek.wzb.eu/pdf/2021/zz21-601.pdf.

Heinze, Anna-Sophie, and Manès Weisskircher. 2022. How Political Parties Respond to Pariah Street Protest: The Case of Anti-Corona Mobilisation in Germany. *German Politics* online first (doi: https://doi.org/10.1080/09644008.2022.2042518).

Kirsch, Peter, Hanno Kube, and Reimut Zohlnhöfer. 2022. Selbstermächtigung: Spaltung der Gesellschaft durch Misstrauen. Forum Marsilius-Kolleg 20: 46–56.

Raisch, Judith, and Reimut Zohlnhöfer. 2020. Beeinflussen Klima-Schulstreiks die politische Agenda? Eine Analyse der Twitterkommunikation von Bundestagsabgeordneten. *Zeitschrift für Parlamentsfragen* 51(3): 667–682.

van Rooij, Benjamin, Anne Leonore de Bruijn, Chris Reinders Folmer, Emmeke Kooistra, Malouke Esra Kuiper, Megan Brownlee, Elke Olthuis, and Adam Fine. 2020. *Compliance with COVID-19 Mitigation Measures in the United States.* Amsterdam: Amsterdam Law School Legal Studies Research Paper No. 2020–21. available at https://doi.org/10.2139/ssrn.3582626.

Corona Self-Empowerment

4

4.1 Data and Method

In this chapter, we discuss the (self-reported) behaviour of the respondents towards the different measures that are supposed to contain the Corona pandemic. For this, we use the index introduced in the previous chapter, which summarises the responses of the respondents to the topics "adhering to the Corona restrictions", "willingness to get vaccinated", "willingness to install the Corona app" and "participation in anti-Corona demonstrations" and can take on values between 0 (perfect Corona compliance) and 14 (complete Corona self-empowerment). Hence, for the following analysis positive coefficients mean that respondents who have the relevant characteristic (to a greater extent) tend to self-empowerment or less compliance in the field of Corona measures. Conversely, a negative sign indicates greater Corona compliance and less self-empowerment.

As explanatory variables, we use several blocks of variables. First, we look at socio-economic variables such as age, gender, education, and employment or status as unemployed or on short-time work. In addition, this block controls for the place of residence in West or East Germany.

Specifically for the Corona measures, we then look at factors that reflect the (subjective) impact of the Corona pandemic. This includes the perceived probability that the respondent or a family member will become infected with the Corona virus in the following two month or such an infection has already occurred. In addition, the respondents should estimate 1) how likely they think it is to be caught by the police or the local authorities if one does not adhere to the Corona restrictions, and 2) how "bad" it would have been for them to be caught. The formulation was deliberately kept open as, in addition to possible penalties, for example, we also wanted to prompt feelings of shame of being caught. In

P. Kirsch et al., *Societal Self-empowerment in Germany*, https://doi.org/10.1007/978-3-658-40865-7_4

addition, we use a question in which the respondents should state whether they consider the restriction of basic rights to contain the pandemic to be justified. Finally, we asked in the second survey how the respondents' economic situation has changed through the Corona pandemic and the efforts to contain it. Since data for this question are only available for the second survey, it cannot be included in the basic models, but it is included in the robustness checks.

We also check whether trust in different political institutions (Bundestag, Federal Government, Federal Constitutional Court, state parliament and state government of the federal state in which the person surveyed lives) as well as in parties, science, public and social media plays a role in the willingness to behave according to the Corona containment strategy of the political decision-makers. The role of satisfaction with the functioning of democracy in Germany is also included. Finally, the answers to the questions of whether the respondents believe that members of the Bundestag try to keep their election promises and that one can trust that the courts effectively protect the rights of citizens against the measures to contain the pandemic also belong to the area of trust.

Another block of factors can be summarized under the heading of self-efficacy. Here we examine whether Corona compliance can be related to the subjective political interest of the respondents, to their perception of being able to influence political decisions themselves, and to their self-assessment of having an insight into the important political problems facing Germany. The latter assessment is also contrasted with the objective knowledge, which is measured by a question about the electoral system of the Federal Republic—as is customary in the literature (Jensen and Zohlnhöfer 2020).

We then look at the role of the respondents' satisfaction with the problem-solving ability of German politics for Corona compliance. The six areas of refugees, pensions, dealing with threats to Germany's security, the Corona pandemic, climate protection and the euro crisis are used for this purpose.

Another block is dedicated to the party preferences of the respondents. Here the parties represented in the 19th German Bundestag, CDU/CSU, SPD, AfD, FDP, Die Linke and Bündnis 90/Die Grünen, other parties and non-voters (but who are allowed to vote) are considered.

In addition, interpersonal trust and conspiracy mentality are analyzed at the individual level. Finally, we look at a variable that we introduced in the previous chapter and that we consider to be an indicator of the acceptance of societal self-empowerment, namely the question of whether one must always follow the law or whether one can follow one's conscience in individual cases.

Finally, a dummy variable is included as a pure control variable, which controls for the survey (summer or winter 2020).

The results reported below are based on regression analyses in which, with few exceptions, all the variables discussed here were included. Occasionally, problems with multicollinearity arise, which can lead to imprecise estimates of coefficients and large standard errors. In particular, the variables measuring trust in the Bundestag and the Federal Government almost always have variance inflation factors of over 10, so that multicollinearity is assumed to be present here. For this reason, these variables were excluded from the calculation of the regressions.

Individual additional variables could not be included in the main models for various reasons. This firstly concerns the variable on the personal economic consequences of the pandemic and its containment, which was only included in the second survey. For party preferences, separate models were estimated for supporters of such parties that at least in principle supported the Corona policy in Germany (CDU/CSU, SPD, FDP, Left, Green), and those who were critical of the Corona policy (AfD, other parties and non-voters). Furthermore, those respondents who answered "Don't know" were excluded from the question of whether one must always adhere to the laws. Since this reduces the number of cases significantly, by around 250 cases, this variable was only integrated in robustness tests. Finally, the dummy variable that maps the wave of the survey produces a significantly positive coefficient. This means that self-empowering behavior with regard to the German decision-makers' containment strategy for Corona was significantly more pronounced in the second observation period (essentially December 2020) than in the first observation period (essentially July 2020). In order to do justice to these differences, separate models were calculated for the two observation periods. Finally, it is examined in each case whether the findings can also be replicated for the individual elements of the self-empowerment index, i.e. compliance with the rules, willingness to be vaccinated and willingness to install the Corona warning app. Separate models for participation in demonstrations are not reported due to the low variance (see Grande et al. 2021 for such an analysis).

The results of the statistical analysis are presented below according to the factor bundles just presented. Even if only the coefficients of the variables relevant for the section are reported in each section, it is always controlled for all other variables. The results of the models are always presented both for both periods together (2,296 respondents) and for the individual periods separately (1,266 respondents for July 2020, 1,030 respondents in December 2020). In order to ensure comparability between the models, the inclusion of the variable on personal economic consequences and acceptance of self-empowerment is always omitted and we controll for the parties that supported the Corona policy of the federal and state governments. Any changes in the results when including the initially excluded variables or the alternative party variables are verbally explained. The results for the variables not initially included in the overall model are of course also reported in the relevant sections. The variance explained by the models is generally good, for the overall period and the second observation period the corrected R^2 is 0.43 in each case, for the first observation period the value is 0.44. This means that our models can explain between 43 and 44% of the variance between the respondents.

4.2 Socio-Economic Factors

We begin our empirical analysis with a number of socio-economic factors. However, before we enter into the empirical analysis, it is necessary to clarify briefly which effects we expect in each case and for what reasons. First of all, it can be assumed that people with an *increasing age* are less likely to self-empower with regard to Corona. On the one hand, this could be because compliance with rules in general should be socially conditioned to a higher degree in older people than in younger people (Dalton 2004, 2015; Norris 1999); on the other hand, infections with the Corona virus become more dangerous with age. If respondents are aware of this, the older ones should adhere to the regulations more strictly and also their willingness to be vaccinated as well as the use of the warning app[1] should be higher (Charron et al. 2022: 13; Vasilopoulos et al. 2022: 11).

With regard to *gender* we have no specific expectations. In contrast, *education* could correlate negatively with Corona self-empowerment, because it is to be expected that the relationships between the measures to contain the pandemic and possible infections will be easier to understand for better educated people. At the same time, however, the opposite effect could be assumed, since it is precisely the well-educated who act as "critical citizens", do not necessarily follow state rules (Ackermann and Zohlnhöfer 2021) and thus also question the Corona measures.

People who are *employed* could be more likely to disregard Corona restrictions than others. This could be because they are more likely to have the opportunity to break the Corona rules (van Rooij et al. 2020: 8), because employment—despite widespread possibilities for home office—offers the necessity to

---

[1] In principle, it could be argued that older people are less technology-oriented and therefore had more difficulty installing and using the app. At least in our sample, which is based on an online survey and thus suggests a minimum level of openness towards digital technology on the part of the respondents, the aspect of protection against infection should predominate.

move outside the home to a greater extent. At work, there are simply more opportunities to violate the rules—e.g. with regard to the obligation to wear masks or
to social distancing during conversations with colleagues. Therefore, this relationship should be observed above all with regard to the actual compliance with
the Corona rules. People who are *unemployed* and in particular *short-time workers* could also be more likely to self-empower with regard to Corona because
they could relate their difficult economic situation to the measures to contain the
pandemic.

Finally, we check whether the respondents live in an *eastern or western
German state*, without having specific expectations for the direction of the
coefficient.

In fact, the consideration of socio-economic factors shows first clear relationships. As expected, the age of the respondents plays an important role in
compliance with the Corona measures. According to our analysis, the willingness to self-empower decreases with age. In other words, older people are more
likely to say that they will comply with the rules, install the app or be vaccinated.
The difference is quite substantial. If we assume the coefficients from model (1)
in Table 4.1 and keep all other variables constant, the difference between an 18-
year-old and an 80-year-old respondent with otherwise identical characteristics
is almost 1.7 points on our 15-point scale—this corresponds to the difference
between "always" and "often" complying with the Corona restrictions.

In contrast, neither the gender of the respondents nor their education plays a
role in Corona compliance, both coefficients are far from statistically significant.
However, at least with regard to gender, the analysis of the aggregated Corona
compliance seems to obscure certain gender differences. If one looks at the self-
reported compliance with rules and willingness to be vaccinated against Corona
separately, there are significant differences between men and women, which, however, point in different directions.[2] While women were significantly more likely
to report that they had complied with the Corona rules (similarly also Anderson
2022: 14; Six et al. 2021: 13; Vasilopoulos et al. 2022: 11), they were, according
to our surveys, more reserved when it came to their willingness to be vaccinated
against Corona. However, these effects were only limited in substance, namely
by around 0.15 points on the underlying five- or six-point scales.

For the labor market situation, however, significant differences can again be
found on the aggregated level. Both persons whowere employed (irrespective
of whether full-time or part-time) and persons who were unemployed or receiving

---

[2] The number of people with diverse gender in our surveys was too small to be taken into
account statistically.

Table 4.1   The influence of socio-economic factors on Corona self-empowerment

	(1) Both surveys	(2) Survey 1	(3) Survey 2
Age	−0.027*** (0.003)	−0.027*** (0.005)	−0.027*** (0.005)
Gender	−0.090 (0.093)	−0.135 (0.127)	−0.022 (0.141)
Education	−0.032 (0.031)	−0.033 (0.042)	−0.035 (0.046)
Employment (Dummy)	0.380*** (0.097)	0.356** (0.128)	0.437** (0.151)
Unemployed or in short-time work (Dummy)	0.612** (.177)	0.360 (0.252)	0.849** (0.255)
West Germany	−0.194 (0.127)	−0.092 (0.168)	−0.303 (0.198)

*Note: The regression coefficients of the variables of interest in this section are given. The models on which the coefficients are based include all the variables discussed in the text. Standard errors in parentheses. * p < 0.05; ** p < 0.01; *** p < 0.001.*

short-time work benefits at the time of the survey showed a significantly higher willingness to self-empowerment than the remaining groups (persons in training, pensioners, housewives and -men). The obvious assumption that employees may possibly comply with the rules less often because they have to go out of the house more often because of work and therefore have more opportunities not to comply with the Corona rules can not be confirmed at first glance: When only the compliance with the Corona rules is analyzed, no significant relationship can be found (nor for unemployed and short-time workers). However, both groups were significantly less willing to be vaccinated and employees also reported using the Corona app less frequently.

We do not find a significant difference in the willingness to self-empowerment between people who live in East and West Germany in our data, neither for the aggregated scale nor for the more specific questions about compliance with the Corona rules or willingness to be vaccinated. Only when it came to downloading the Corona app, people in East Germany seemed to be more hesitant.

The reported relationships remain unchanged for the joint investigation of both surveys if, instead of support for parties that fundamentally support the Corona policy of the German decision-makers, one controls for the skeptical parties or if the variable for the acceptance of self-empowerment is included.

Even if the two surveys are evaluated separately from each other, the results remain stable overall. Only the coefficient of unemployed or short-time workers loses statistical significance when restricting the sample to the first survey—possibly because the loss of employment or short-time work was only recently and initially considered to be short-term. In addition, the variable gender just misses statistical significance in the investigation of the willingness to vaccinate in the first survey (p = 0.062), but in this survey there is a significant effect with regard to the use of the Corona warning app: According to this, men were more willing than women to use the app at an early stage in July 2020. The significance of the coefficients for employees and unemployed/short-time workers also disappears in the analysis of the first survey when the willingness to vaccinate and the Corona app are examined. In addition, the differences between East and West Germans in the use of the Corona app lose their significance when the first period is considered separately.

Overall, it can be concluded that self-empowerment in the context of Corona decreases with age and increases with participation in the labour market (whether in employment or as unemployed or on short-time work). Education seems—somewhat surprisingly—not to play a role, while gender is associated with different behaviour in different areas. While, according to our data, men are more willing to be vaccinated than women, women, on the other hand, have complied more with the Corona rules than men.

4.3 Affectedness by the Pandemic and the Measures to Combat it

The willingness to comply with the Corona restrictions should also have to do with how strongly the respondents are affected by the pandemic and its economic and social consequences. Obviously, people who consider it very likely that they or relatives will *become infected* should comply with the Corona measures to a greater extent than people who consider an infection unlikely (cf. also Erhardt et al. 2021; Jørgensen et al. 2021; Six et al. 2021 as well as Vasilopoulos et al. 2022). We look at deterrence effects with questions about the perceived probability of *being caught* when violating the Corona restrictions and the perception of *how serious a possible discovery* is (cf. van Rooij et al. 2020: 7). The more likely it appears that a violation of a Corona regulation will be discovered, and the worse such a discovery is, the more likely the respondents will comply with the rules. However, this should apply above all to the question of compliance with the Corona rules, while downloading the Corona warning app and vaccinations were not compulsory and the right to demonstrate of course continued. The willingness to comply with rules should also be more pronounced the more these *rules are perceived as justified*—in particular if they interfere with basic rights. Rules are probably seen as justified above all if the respondent believes that they work and the benefits outweigh the costs. Therefore, we expect that respondents who consider the interference with basic rights to be justified will be less likely to act on their own authority with regard to Corona. Finally, people whose *economic situation* has deteriorated as a result of the crisis may be less willing to comply with the rules that they may hold (partly) responsible for their economic difficulties (similarly Six et al. 2021: 6).

We begin with the influence of the perceived probability that the respondents themselves or a family member will become infected with the Corona virus within the following two months (note that persons who or whose relatives already got infected with Corona were assigned the maximum value plus 1). It becomes clear that people who expect an infection are much more willing to comply with the Corona restrictions than people who consider an infection unlikely. The difference is substantial: Let us compare two people with the same values for all other characteristics, but one of whom considered it absolutely unlikely that they or a relative would become infected, while the other considered an infection within the next two months to be absolutely likely. Model 4 in Table 4.2 predicts a self-empowerment value that is 0.8 scale points higher for the person who considers infection unlikely—for example, the difference between always and mostly complying with the restrictions. Somewhat surprisingly, there are significant differences in the disaggregated view of the individual components of our self-empowerment index for this variable. In fact, the perceived probability of infection is highly relevant for the willingness to be vaccinated and the willingness to use the Corona app, but not for the general compliance with the Corona rules.

In contrast, the perceived probability of being caught violating the Corona restrictions has no significant effect on Corona self-empowerment—at least at the aggregate level. If one looks only at the self-reported compliance with the Corona restrictions, the expected negative effect can also be found for this variable: People who consider it likely to be caught violating the rules therefore comply significantly more with the rules. However, this effect is rather small. Not surprisingly, the probability of being discovered plays no role for vaccination

Table 4.2 The influence of being affected on Corona self-empowerment

	(4) Both surveys	(5) Survey 1	(6) Survey 2
Probability of infection	−0.042*** (0.008)	−0.038** (0.011)	−0.048*** (0.013)
Probability of being caught for violations	0.003 (0.002)	0.001 (0.003)	0.006 (0.003)
How bad would it be to get caught	−0.008*** (0.002)	−0.008** (0.002)	−0.010*** (0.003)
Perception, restrictions are justified	−0.028*** (0.002)	−0.029*** (0.003)	−0.026*** (0.003)
Economic situation (†)	Not available	Not available	−0.002 (0.004)

*Note: The regression coefficients of the variables of interest in this section are shown. The models on which the coefficients are based include all the variables discussed in the text. Standard errors in parentheses. ** $p < 0.01$; *** $p < 0.001$. (†) The models are always estimated without the variable "Economic situation", even in this section. Therefore, the regression coefficient for this variable comes from another estimation than the other coefficients.*

readiness and the use of the Corona app[3]—both of which were not mandatory for citizens and therefore the discovery does not play a role.

The situation is different when it comes to the question of how "bad" it would be for respondents if they were discovered breaking the rules. Here we see a significantly negative relationship with Corona self-empowerment, which substantively corresponds approximately to the size of the effect of the perceived infection risk: If we keep all other variables constant again, Model 4 in Table 4.2 results in a difference of 0.8 points on our 15-point scale between a person for whom discovery would not be bad at all and a person for whom this would be extremely bad. When looking at the individual elements of Corona policy, it becomes apparent that this variable is only irrelevant for vaccination willingness.

The next item was asked much more abstractly, namely whether the respondents consider the restrictions on basic rights to protect against the pandemic to be justified or not. As expected, we receive a highly significant negative coefficient. This means that the more people considered the restrictions to be justified, the more willing they were to comply with the various measures. The perception that the restrictions are justified also has a substantively considerable effect.

---

[3] The perceived probability of being caught has even a significantly negative effect on the willingness to install the Corona app.

If we compare identical persons again, but one of them does not consider the measures to be justified at all, while the other considers them to be completely justified, Model 4 in Table 4.2 predicts a difference of almost three scale points—the difference between people who "always" and only "sometimes" complied with the restrictions. This effect also remains in the disaggregated analysis of the individual elements of the Corona measures.

The reported results remain unchanged when controlling for support for other parties or the general willingness to follow laws when considering the overall sample and the data from the first survey. Results change for the second survey when looking at the perceived probability of being caught by the police or the local authority when violating the law. In the aggregate view, the coefficient is now significantly positive when controlling for the question of whether one should always obey the law. In addition, the coefficient for this variable loses its significance when restricted to compliance with Corona rules. When looking at the use of the Corona app alone for the second survey, the variable that reflects how bad discovery would be for those affected also loses its significance.

The particularly interesting thing about the separate consideration of the second survey in this section is, however, above all that an additional question about the change in the respondents' economic situation through the pandemic and the efforts to contain it can be used. While the other variables of interest in this section remain substantively unchanged, the expected significant effect does not materialize for the respondents' economic situation: People whose economic situation, according to their own perception, has worsened as a result of the pandemic, do not tend to self-empower more than others. At least in the disaggregated analysis, there is a significant effect for the willingness to be vaccinated. People who have suffered economic damage as a result of Corona would therefore be more likely to get vaccinated—possibly in order to overcome the crisis situation quickly.

In summary, it can be said that the perceived individual impact of the pandemic—whether through the risk of infection or the changed personal economic situation—has had an impact on Corona self-empowerment. However, the effects of both forms of impact are not significant, especially when it comes to self-reported compliance with Corona regulations. The probability of being discovered and the perception of a possible discovery as bad are of greater importance for the latter. There is empirical evidence that the amount of the possible fine played a role in the perception of the respondents as to how bad it is to be caught. A correlation between the minimum amount of the fines for the violation of the mask requirement in the federal states and the average proportion of the respondents in the federal states who would have found it bad to be caught in our first survey results in a moderate correlation coefficient of $r = 0.457$, which is statistically significant at the 10 percent level. However, the most substantively important variable in this section is the perception that the restrictions were justified.

4.4   Trust in Institutions and Actors

In the literature, it has been pointed out time and again how important *political trust* is for compliance with the rules (e.g. Marien and Hooghe 2011; Citrin and Stoker 2018); this is especially true for the assessment of and compliance with the Corona rules, which have been linked to political trust in a number of contributions (as a first overview see Devine et al. 2021; see also, for example, Altiparmakis et al. 2021; Bargain and Aminjonov 2020; Charron et al. 2022; Jäckle et al. 2022; Jørgensen et al. 2021; Seyd and Bu 2022; Six et al. 2021; Vasilopoulos et al. 2022). We expect that trust in political institutions, science and the media, satisfaction with democracy and the expectation that politicians will try to keep their election promises, as well as the effective protection of fundamental rights by the courts, will also have a positive effect on the willingness to comply with and implement the Corona measures. For example, citizens who trust the German Bundestag and the Federal Government or the state parliament and state government of their federal state should be more willing to accept legal acts passed by these institutions or to follow recommendations made by these institutions, as they assume that these decision-makers generally try to find the best possible solutions to problems for the community (see, for example, Charron et al. 2022: 7). The same applies to political parties as the key actors in political decision-making processes. The question of whether respondents believe that politicians try to implement their election promises is also a dimension of trust, namely trust in the functioning of representative democracy. Finally, the question of satisfaction with the actual functioning of democracy in Germany also provides information on the respondents' democratic trust (Citrin and Stoker 2018: 51), because those who are satisfied with the actual functioning of democracy in Germany—not just with the idea of democracy—are likely to have trust in the democracy that functions in this way.

In addition to democratic trust, *trust in the rule of law* could also play a role. We measure this dimension by asking about trust in the Federal Constitutional Court, but also by asking respondents whether they trust that the courts will effectively protect the rights of citizens against the far-reaching measures to contain the Corona pandemic. Again, we expect that people who have such trust in the rule of law will be less prone to self-empowerment, because they expect that there may be limits to state interventions in their civil liberties.

Finally, *trust in the media and science* could play a role. Especially in the fight against the Corona pandemic, politics was to a considerable extent dependent on the findings of science. In order to contain the pandemic and to decide which measures should be taken, it was crucial to understand how the virus is transmitted, which distances should be kept, which masks promise protection or which vaccines are suitable for which groups of people. Therefore, it can be expected that people who trust in science were more willing to accept measures that should implement (often provisional) scientific results politically. This should apply in particular to the willingness to be vaccinated, as of course there were no long-term experiences for the vaccines developed in the shortest possible time.

Just as important could be the trust in the media. Depending on the information citizens receive about the pandemic, they will be more or less willing to comply with the Corona rules. For example, those who frequent blogs or social media channels from the Corona skeptic "Querdenker" scene will probably think differently about the Corona pandemic and the need for certain measures than people who read quality daily newspapers. In the following, we focus on the trust in public service broadcasting as the medium with the largest reach, which probably distributed objective information about the pandemic. Therefore, we expect that trust in public service broadcasting should be associated with higher Corona compliance. In contrast, we examine the influence of an additive index for social media, which reflects the trust in information from blogs, Youtube, Facebook and other platforms. For this indicator, we expect an effect that increases self-empowerment.

The empirical results from Table 4.3 can only confirm the theoretical considerations presented above to a limited extent. In line with our expectations, we find that people who trust in science and public service broadcasting tend to be less self-empowering than others. Substantially, this represents a difference of almost 0.6 (science) or 0.8 (public service broadcasting) points on our 15-point scale. The coefficient for trust in social media, which has a positive sign and thus signals a self-empowering effect of trust in information from blogs, Youtube, Twitter etc., barely reaches statistical significance ($p = 0.069$).

Looking at the individual elements of Corona compliance, it can be seen that trust in science—not surprisingly—is particularly important for willingness to be vaccinated. Trust in public service broadcasting promotes both the willingness to install the Corona app and the willingness to be vaccinated. Interestingly, trust is associated with higher compliance in areas where voluntariness prevails in both cases, while neither trust in public service broadcasting nor trust in science has an

Table 4.3   The influence of trust on Corona self-empowerment

	(7) Both surveys	(8) Survey 1	(9) Survey 2
Trust in Parliament	0.042 (0.023)	0.017 (0.031)	0.073* (0.036)
Trust in government	0.002 (0.022)	−0.007 (0.028)	0.019 (0.034)
Trust in parties	−0.027 (0.017)	−0.022 (0.023)	−0.032 (0.024)
Politicians try to keep promises	0.002 (0.014)	−0.003 (0.019)	0.001 (0.022)
Democracy Satisfaction	−0.004 (0.003)	−0.006 (0.004)	−0.004 (0.004)
Trust in Federal Constitutional Court	−0.003 (0.015)	−0.004 (0.020)	−0.008 (0.022)
Courts protect effectively	−0.019 (0.011)	−0.039* (0.016)	0.007 (0.017)
Trust in Science	−0.031* (0.014)	−0.012 (0.020)	−0.056** (0.021)
Trust in public broadcasting	−0.039** (0.012)	−0.035* (0.015)	−0.043* (0.018)
Trust in social media	0.007 (0.004)	0.015** (0.005)	−0.003 (0.006)

Note: The regression coefficients of the variables of interest in this section are given. The models on which the coefficients are based include all the variables discussed in the text. Standard errors in parentheses. $* p < 0.05$; $** p < 0.01$.

impact on compliance with formal Corona restrictions. Things are different when it comes to trust in social media in the wider sense. For this variable, one obtains a significantly positive coefficient when investigating self-empowerment in relation to compliance with Corona restrictions. This means that people who trust information from social media have systematically complied less with Corona regulations than people who have little trust in new media.

A look at the differences between the two surveys shows that the relevance of trust in science has increased over time: Table 4.3 shows that in summer 2020 trust in science was not yet significantly associated with self-empowerment in the Corona area—which is probably due to the fact that in the first survey, the relationship between trust in science and willingness to be vaccinated was not yet significant. In the following winter, perhaps as a result of the discussion about vaccines to be introduced soon, both coefficients then become significant. Trust in public broadcasting is also not significantly associated with the use of the Corona app in the first survey. In contrast, in the first survey, the coefficient for trust in social media is significantly positive. Instead, the negative effect of trust in social media on compliance with Corona regulations weakens in the second survey, so that the coefficient loses its statistical significance. At the same time, trust in social media in the second survey even leads to an increased willingness to use the Corona app.

In contrast, all variables that are supposed to reflect the respondents' democratic or rule-of-law trust remain far from statistical significance, in some cases not even the signs go in the expected direction. This is essentially also the case when the individual surveys are evaluated separately. The significantly positive coefficient for trust in the state parliament in the second survey not only goes in the opposite direction to expectations, but the significance also disappears when controlling for the acceptance of self-empowerment. This leaves only one coefficient that meets theoretical expectations: People who believe that one can trust that the courts will also effectively protect fundamental rights under pandemic conditions were significantly less likely to engage in Corona self-empowerment in the first survey.

Even if the individual items of Corona compliance are examined separately, little support is found for the importance of democratic or rule-of-law trust. Nevertheless, both in the consideration of both surveys and in the separate examination of the second survey, it can be seen that satisfaction with democracy in Germany is significantly associated with compliance with Corona regulations: The more satisfied people are with the functioning of democracy in Germany, the more willing they were to comply with the Corona restrictions. In addition, in all surveys trust in political parties was positively associated with willingness to be vaccinated and trust in the courts increased willingness to install the Corona warning app in the first survey.

However, the low number of significant results for the variables measuring democratic and rule-of-law trust is probably not due to the actual lack of substantial relationships, but rather to the high correlation between the individual variables measuring trust, as well as between these variables and the variables measuring the perception of the state's ability to solve problems. The variables measuring democratic trust (satisfaction with democracy, trust in the Bundestag, federal government, state parliament, state government, expectation that politicians will implement election promises) are extremely highly correlated with each other.[4] The correlation between the two variables measuring rule-of-law trust (trust in the Federal Constitutional Court and effective protection of fundamental rights by courts) is also high ($r = 0.627$). Finally, the variables measuring democratic and rule-of-law trust are also highly correlated (in the case of the Bundestag and the Federal Constitutional Court, the correlation is as high as $r = 0.806$), and even the variables measuring trust and the variables measuring the political system's ability to solve problems are closely interrelated (with the exception of climate protection).

If independent variables are highly correlated with each other, this leads to the problem of multicollinearity, which in turn leads to a inadequate estimation of both the coefficients and the standard errors. This can possibly lead to the affected coefficients not being significant. That is why we had originally excluded the variables measuring trust in the Bundestag and federal government from the regression, because the variance inflation factor for these variables had shown values of over 10. But the very high correlations, exceeding the limit of $r = 0.7$ in 20 cases, indicate that multicollinearity is also a problem for the variables measuring democratic and rule-of-law trust.[5]

Therefore, in a further step, we estimated regressions in which all variables were included except those measuring trust and perceived problem-solving ability. Subsequently, a single trust variable was included in each regression. It turns out that, with the exception of trust in the state parliament and in keeping election promises, we find significant coefficients with the expected sign for all variables. In addition, we computed an additive index from the variables measuring trust in the rule of law and from the core variables measuring trust in democracy (trust in the Bundestag, federal government, parties, state government, democracy satisfaction) and, since these indices are still highly correlated with each other ($r = 0.791$), included them separately in the regression. In both cases, we find significant relationships in the expected direction. For example, people with pronounced democratic trust have, ceteris paribus, a self-empowerment value for Corona measures that is just under one point lower than people with very little democratic trust. For trust in the rule of law, the difference is just under 0.6 points.

In a further step, we additionally included an indicator in the regression which additively maps satisfaction with problem-solving ability across all six policy areas surveyed. Again, only one trust variable was added. In these regressions,

---

[4] The lowest correlation coefficient between two variables measuring democratic trust is $r = 0.616$ (satisfaction with democracy – election promises), the highest is $r = 0.940$ (Bundestag – federal government) and $r = 0.926$ (state parliament – state government).

[5] The other results reported in this chapter are not affected, they remain unchanged even if the variables measuring trust and the ability to solve problems are omitted.

we find that, with increasing satisfaction with democracy and increasing trust in the Bundestag, self-empowerment in relation to Corona measures decreased, the same applies to the index of democratic trust. Similarly, trust in the Federal Constitutional Court and in the willingness of courts to protect fundamental rights even in times of Corona, individually as well as in the form of the additive index, leads to higher acceptance of Corona measures.

The results for democratic and rule of law trust remain essentially identical even when the individual surveys are analysed separately. In particular, if the perception of political problem-solving ability is not controlled for, the coefficients for democracy satisfaction, trust in the Bundestag and Federal Constitutional Court as well as in courts and the two additive indices remain significantly negative (exception: courts in the second survey and index of rule of law trust). If, in addition, the perception of problem-solving ability is included, the reported effects at least remain for the first survey.

Finally, if we look at the individual elements of our self-empowerment index separately, we find a significant negative effect on violations of Corona rules for satisfaction with democracy, but not for the other variables. All variables are much more successful, however, when it comes to the use of the Corona warning app and willingness to be vaccinated. However, it is noteworthy that the results for the second survey are less clear.

One possible explanation for the surprisingly diverse findings for trust variables could be that trust is not always relevant for self-empowerment. It has been argued in various places that political trust only influences compliance when respondents do not have great fear (cf. Seyd and Bu 2022 as well as Vasilopoulos et al. 2022): If a person has a significant fear of possible infection, they will comply with the rules—regardless of whether they trust political decision-makers or not. Only when the fear subsides, that is, when there are subjectively fewer incentives for norm-based behavior, does trust become important. People who are not afraid of infection but have political trust should then still not tend to self-empower, while people who are not afraid of infection and report little political trust should self-empower more.

This expectation can be empirically tested using Fig. 4.1. The figure is based on the regression for both periods underlying this chapter; however, all variables measuring political trust were replaced by the index of democratic trust; the problem-solving variables were included individually. What the figure shows is the marginal effect of democratic trust on self-empowerment at different levels of fear of infection. The solid line shows the estimated effect, the dashed lines give the 95% confidence interval. The figure shows that the effect of democratic trust on Corona self-empowerment is significantly negative for people who con-sider it very unlikely to get infected—the confidence intervals do not include the zero line. This means that for people with low concern about infection, demo-cratic trust plays a significant role in whether they self-empower or not. However, from a moderate perceived probability of infection, the confidence interval also includes the zero line, hence, the effect becomes insignificant. This means that for people with moderate or even high perceived probability of infection, democratic trust no longer plays a role.

In summary, it can be argued that the different aspects of political trust play an important role in understanding societal self-empowerment in the context of Corona measures. Democratic trust and, in particular, satisfaction with the con-crete functioning of democracy in Germany have a clearly dampening effect on all aspects of self-empowerment. This is especially true for people who were not very worried about becoming infected with the virus. Similar considerations

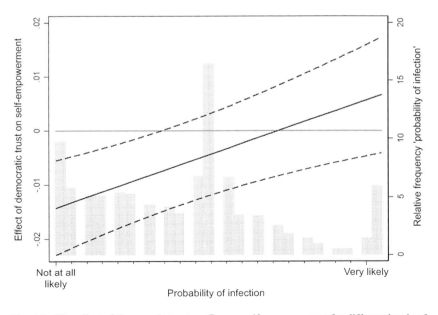

Fig. 4.1 The effect of democratic trust on Corona self-empowerment for different levels of fear of infection. (Source: own representation. Thanks to Fabian Engler for the creation of the figure)

apply to rule of law trust, which, however, affects primarily the voluntary elements of the Corona measures, namely the use of the Corona app and willingness to be vaccinated, but not the actual compliance with the Corona restrictions. In these two areas, trust in public service broadcasting also has a particularly strong counteracting effect on self-empowerment. The same is especially true when considering willingness to be vaccinated for trust in science. In contrast, people who trust social media seem to have paid less attention to the Corona rules.

4.5 Self-Efficacy

Next, we turn to the influence of perceived self-efficacy on Corona self-empowerment. Under self-efficacy, we subsume a number of indicators that are intended to capture, on the one hand, whether the person concerned feels able to *understand political connections* ("good insight into the important political problems") and, on the other hand, whether she has a minimum level of *political knowledge* (significance of the first and second vote in federal elections). We assume that people who subjectively feel well informed about politics or have a certain level of knowledge about the political system are less likely to self-empower in relation to the Corona measures because they better understand the connection between the problem of the pandemic and the measures taken in response to it.[6] For this reason, we also expect that people who are *interested in politics* will accept the measures to contain the virus more readily than those who are not interested in politics. On the other hand, we assume that people who believe that they *cannot influence political decisions* may be more prone to Corona self-empowerment. Precisely because they do not believe that they can assert their interests through the political process, they might be tempted to express their protest by not complying with the rules.

We find no immediate confirmation for any of the variables examined in this section, although many coefficients just barely miss statistical significance. This is the case, for example, for the negative influence of political interest on Corona self-empowerment (p = 0.052). However, if one additionally controls for the acceptance of self-empowerment, the coefficient jumps over the significance threshold. This means that people who state that they are interested in politics are more likely to follow the Corona measures. However, this effect is relatively

---

[6] However, the opposite hypothesis has also been put forward in the literature, but has not been empirically confirmed: According to this, people who think they are well informed about political issues would be more critical of the measures to combat the pandemic and therefore less willing to comply with the restrictions (Kestilä-Kekkonen et al. 2022).

Table 4.4   The influence of self-efficacy on Corona self-empowerment

	(10) Both surveys	(11) Survey 1	(12) Survey 2
Political interest	−0.004	−0.006*	−0.002
	(0,002)	(0.003)	(0.003)
No influence on government	0.013	0.015	0.009
	(0.008)	(0.011)	(0.012)
Insights into political problems	0.007	0.016	−0.002
	(0.012)	(0.016)	(0.018)
Political knowledge	−0.116	−0.187	−0.036
	(0.095)	(0.129)	(0.142)

*Note: The regression coefficients of the variables of interest in this section are given. The models on which the coefficients are based include all the variables discussed in the text. Standard errors in parentheses. * p <0.05;.*

weak. If we use the coefficients from Model 10 in Table 4.4 as a basis, the difference between someone who is not interested in politics at all and someone who is extremely interested in politics, with otherwise identical characteristics, does not even make half a point on our 15-point scale of self-empowerment. In addition, the effect of political interest is no longer present when we only examine compliance with Corona regulations. On the other hand, political interest is associated with a higher probability of installing the Corona app and getting vaccinated.

People who believe that they can't influence what the government does actually have no significantly higher inclination towards self-empowerment than other respondents. Although the coefficient has the expected positive sign, it just barely misses (again) the usual levels of significance (p = 0.094). Including the question of whether one must always adhere to the law doesn't change anything. However, the separate analysis of the use of the Corona app shows that people who believe that they can't influence the government's actions are less likely to use the app.

Even the coefficients for the variables measuring the perception of having a good insight oneself into the most important problems in Germany, as well as the "objective" political knowledge, measured by a question about the importance of the first and second vote in federal elections, fail to reach statistical significance and can therefore not explain differences in the inclination towards Corona self-empowerment—regardless of whether the inclination towards general compliance is controlled for or not.

If we look at the two surveys separately, we find that political interest in the first survey is also significantly associated with the acceptance of self-empowerment without controlling for the willingness to comply with the law. Moreover, the variable just barely misses ($p = 0.060$) statistical significance for the use of the Corona app. Similarly, we find that for people who do not believe that they have influence on government decisions, there is no significant effect on the use of the Corona app when we look at the surveys separately, but they do comply significantly less with the Corona restrictions in the first survey, even if we control for the idea that one must always adhere to the law. Political knowledge has a positive effect on the use of the app in the first survey. When we look only at the data from the second survey, the significance of the variable political interest is lost both when we look at the aggregate and when we look at the willingness to be vaccinated, while at the same time it is significantly associated with higher compliance with the Corona rules.

In summary, it can be said that self-efficacy and political knowledge have only limited explanatory potential for Corona self-empowerment. With some caution, it can be said that people who are interested in politics are less likely to engage in self-empowerment with regard to Corona measures. In addition, there are isolated indications that people who have low political self-efficacy, i.e. those who do not believe that they can influence government decisions, are more likely to engage in self-empowerment with regard to Corona measures—but, according to our data, this is by no means a consistent pattern.

4.6   Problem-Solving Ability of the Political System

Political systems have the central task of solving collective problems. Therefore, it can be expected that the perception of citizens, whether their political system provides this service, is of central importance for the willingness to submit to the rules of this system. If people come to the conclusion that the government does not solve central problems, this could lead them to no longer regard the rules as binding for them (Anderson 2022: 6)—they could empower themselves.

We would like to check this possibility by linking the satisfaction of the respondents with the performance of the federal government in different central areas with the inclination to Corona self-empowerment. On the one hand, we have identified the crises that have occupied voters strongly in recent electoral periods as core policy areas: the euro crisis, the refugee crisis and the Corona crisis itself. On the other hand, we have included central further policy areas that have played a role in recent years, namely climate policy, pensions and the handling of threats to Germany's security.

Empirically, a very nuanced picture emerges: In fact, it is not the satisfaction with the problem-solving in all policy areas that is equally relevant for the willingness to Corona self-empowerment. Rather, it is—not surprisingly—the satisfaction with the management of the Corona pandemic that plays a special role. The less satisfied a person is with Corona policy, the less willing they are to support the measures envisaged by the governments. A person who is very satisfied with Corona policy would therefore have a value that is lower by just under one point on our Corona self-empowerment scale than a very dissatisfied person under otherwise equal conditions. In contrast, the coefficient for satisfaction with the handling of threats to Germany's security points in the opposite direction. The more satisfied people are with this policy, the more likely they are to empower themselves in Corona matters—a result that cannot be immediately explained plausibly.

Due to the high correlation of the variables measuring trust and problem-solving discussed above and the resulting problem of multicollinearity, another regression was estimated excluding the trust variables.[7] The results for the variables of interest in this section remain largely unchanged, with one important exception: Now it turns out that also people who are dissatisfied with the euro rescue policy tend to Corona self-empowerment. Satisfaction with pension, climate and refugee policy, on the other hand, has no significant impact on Corona compliance.

When considering the individual elements of the Corona measures, the great importance of satisfaction with Corona policy becomes apparent once again: For both the willingness to be vaccinated and the willingness to use the Corona app (but not for compliance with the rules), there are significantly negative coefficients that suggest that the inclination to Corona self-empowerment decreases with increasing satisfaction with Corona policy. For satisfaction with the handling of security threats, only a positive effect on the willingness to be vaccinated was found. If thetrust variables are omitted, we also find that satisfaction with the Euro crisis policy is associated with increased willingness to be vaccinated.

Over time, few changes can be found, as the comparison between models 14 and 15 in Table 4.5 shows. The most relevant factor in both surveys is satisfaction with Corona policy, while the—already unexpected—positive effect on the

---

[7] Although the variables that map the satisfaction with the problem-solving ability in different policy areas are also relatively highly correlated with each other, since there is no correlation above r = 0.7, they can all be included.

question of Germany's threats turns out to be not completely robust, as it loses its significance when the two surveys are examined separately. Conversely, the negative effect of satisfaction with Euro rescue policy was only found again in the separate examination of the first survey, and only if the trust variables were excluded and, in addition, it was controlled for the assessment that one always has to comply with the law (acceptance of self-empowerment). For the separate examination of the individual elements of the Corona measures in the different surveys, it becomes apparent that in the first survey satisfaction with Corona policy was also not significantly related to the use of the app.

According to the findings of this section, it can be concluded that satisfaction with Corona policy is an important factor for compliance with most aspects of Corona policy. This is certainly not entirely surprising, but still interesting. This means that compliance is less likely to be the case for those who do not agree with the rules. The finding that people who are dissatisfied (satisfied) with the handling of threats to Germany's security are more (less) likely to comply with Corona rules is unexpected and requires further investigation. In fact, this relationship seems to exist primarily in terms of willingness to vaccinate. Finally, there are scattered indications that dissatisfaction with Euro rescue policy could have fueled Corona self-empowerment.

Table 4.5 The influence of the perception of the political system's ability to solve problems on Corona self-empowerment

	(13) Both surveys	(14) Survey 1	(15) Survey 2
Refugee policy	0.016 (0.011)	0.010 (0.015)	0.030 (0.018)
Social security for the elderly	−0.010 (0.012)	−0.003 (0.016)	−0.015 (0.019)
Threats to Germany's security	0.032** (0.012)	0.032 (0.017)	0.031 (0.019)
Corona pandemic	−0.047*** (0.013)	−0.040* (0.018)	−0.055** (0.019)
Climate change	−0.001 (0.012)	0.008 (0.016)	−0.015 (0.018)
Euro crisis	−0.016 (0.013)	−0.009 (0.018)	−0.020 (0.020)

*Note: The regression coefficients of the variables of interest in this section are given. The models on which the coefficients are based include all the variables discussed in the text. Standard errors in parentheses. *p<0.05 ** p < 0.01; *** p < 0.001.*

4.7   Party Preferences

In a next step, we investigate to what extent party preferences influence self-empowerment with regard to Corona. It is to be expected that people who are close to the parties that at the time of the surveys formed the federal government (*CDU/CSU and SPD*) will tend less to self-empowering behavior, since it was precisely the parties closest to them that set the course for the Corona measures (cf. also Altiparmakis et al. 2021: 1166; Anderson 2022: 6; Charron et al. 2022). The same should apply to the supporters of *Alliance 90/The Greens.* On the one hand, the consent of the Greens in the Bundesrat was necessary for the adoption of the (few) relevant federal laws (e.g. the various Population Protection Acts), so that voters of this party could have assumed that the ideas of "their" party are also reflected to a sufficient extent in the laws. On the other hand, the great role of federal interlocking policymaking and, in particular, the Conference of the Prime Ministers of the German states, is to be taken into account (cf. Behnke 2020; Person et al. i. E.). The fact that almost all important decisions on combating the pandemic had to be implemented by the respective state governments and that the Greens were represented in the majority of state governments is likely to have been another signal for supporters of the Greens to accept the regulations. This argument applies in a somewhat weakened form to *FDP* and *Linke,* which were each involved in three state governments during the observation period (FDP in North Rhine-Westphalia, Rhineland-Palatinate and Schleswig-Holstein, Linke in Berlin, Bremen and—as the leading party—in Thuringia). However, since the latter parties were presumably much less able to influence Corona policy, and in particular the FDP took quite critical positions (cf. also Chap. 6), the supporters of these parties should also less clearly support the Corona measures.

On the other hand, the *AfD* positioned itself more and more strongly as a critic of the Corona policy of the federal government and the federal states as the pandemic progressed. At the same time, it was not involved in the federal or a state government. This rejection of the Corona measures could have encouraged AfD voters to conclude that they were entitled to act on their own with regard to Corona and not to comply with the rules. Something similar could be assumed for supporters of parties that are not represented in the Bundestag (and usually in a state parliament) and therefore had no influence on Corona policy. Finally, non-voters could also have felt unrepresented in German Corona policy, which could also have been associated with a higher tendency to self-empowerment.

As already explained above, for methodological reasons not all parties can be included in the regressions at the same time. Therefore, two—otherwise identical—models were computed, in one of which only the parties were included whose support should theoretically go hand in hand with the acceptance of the Corona measures, while in the second model the preferences for the AfD, other parties and non-voting were taken into account.

These theoretical expectations are confirmed empirically overall (Table 4.6). We begin with the discussion of the established and involved parties in the formulation of the Corona policy. The support of these parties is associated with a significantly lower willingness to engage in self-empowering behavior in the Corona pandemic. The only exception here is the FDP, for whose followers the coefficient is not significant—but this fits quite well with the party's rather critical attitude towards the Corona policy (Engler and Zohlnhöfer i. E.; s. Kap. 6). It is interesting that the two opposition parties, the Greens and the Left, have the largest coefficients, while the support of the governing party SPD is only relatively weakly associated with willingness to Corona compliance—indeed, if one controls for the acceptance of self-empowerment, the SPD coefficient even loses its statistical significance (p = 0.075).

It is also interesting that the significance of all these coefficients, with the exception of that for the Left, is lost when considering compliance with Corona rules and vaccination readiness separately.

If one looks at the preference for established parties separately for the two surveys, it becomes apparent that in summer 2020, SPD supporters no longer reported significantly higher compliance with rules than the other respondents. Otherwise, the findings for the first survey remain largely unchanged compared to the aggregate consideration of both surveys.[8] In the second survey, however, the significance of the coefficients has largely disappeared. Only the supporters of the Left still showed a significantly lower tendency towards self-empowerment. The coefficients for an intention to vote for the Greens and—quite remarkably— the FDP just missed the usual levels of significance (p = 0.062 and 0.079), while the coefficients for the voters of the two governing parties are clearly far from significance. If one takes the variable for the acceptance of self-empowerment into the regression, the coefficients of all parties become clearly insignificant. Finally, if one looks at the effects of the intention to vote on the individual components of Corona compliance in winter 2020, one finds significant effects only for the willingness to install the Corona app: Accordingly, supporters of CDU/CSU and Greens were significantly more willing than the others to download the app.

On the aggregate level for both surveys, one also finds mainly the expected results for the intention to vote for the AfD, other non-established parties and

---

[8] Only the coefficient for the Left loses significance in the separate consideration of willingness to be vaccinated and use of the Corona app.

Table 4.6 The influence of party preferences on Corona self-empowerment

	(16) Both surveys	(17) Survey 1	(18) Survey 2
CDU/CSU	−0.471** (0.135)	−0.536** (0.181)	−0.316 (0.208)
SPD	−0.356* (0.164)	−0.404 (0.228)	−0.245 (0.241)
FDP	−0.304 (0.216)	−0.081 (0.285)	−0.587 (0.333)
The Left	−0.619** (0.179)	−0.538* (0.237)	−0.606* (0.279)
Alliance 90/The Greens	−0.610*** (0.154)	−0.678** (0.206)	−0.442 (0.236)
AfD (†)	*0.680*** (0.169)*	*0.630** (0.221)*	*0.725** (0.266)*
Other party (†)	*0.282 (0.181)*	*0.477 (0.258)*	*0.049 (0.258)*
Non-voters (†)	*0.460** (0.145)*	*0.369 (0.193)*	*0.474* (0.223)*

*Note: The regression coefficients of the variables of interest in this section are given. The models on which the coefficients are based include all the variables discussed in the text. Standard errors in parentheses. * p < 0.05; ** p < 0.01; *** p < 0.001. (†) Not all intention-to-vote variables could be included in a regression equation. The intention to vote for AfD, other parties and non-voting was therefore included separately from the intention to vote for the established parties.*

non-voters. Both the intention to vote for the AfD and the intention not to participate in the next election go hand in hand with a greater willingness to self-empowerment in Corona matters—regardless of whether one controls for the acceptance of self-empowerment or not. In contrast, the intention to vote for another non-established party has no statistically significant effect. When the individual Corona measures are analyzed separately, the self-empowerment of AfD supporters and non-voters in Corona matters is primarily reflected in the willingness not to use the Corona warning app. Neither the AfD voting intention nor the intention not to vote plays a role in compliance with the Corona rules and willingness to be vaccinated.

If one differentiates between the two surveys, one also finds the AfD effect for the first survey on the aggregate level, while the coefficient for the intention not to vote just misses the threshold of statistical significance (p = 0.056). In summer 2020, the intention to vote for the AfD also only very narrowly missed having a self-empowerment-enhancing effect on compliance with Corona measures (p = 0.053).

In summary, it can be concluded that the intention to vote does indeed have an effect on Corona compliance. In principle, voters of the established parties, who were also involved in the formulation of Corona policy, seem to be more willing to implement the corresponding measures themselves—although this does not apply to potential voters of the FDP and applies above all to the use of the Corona app. On the other hand, supporters of the AfD and people who do not vote tend to act on their own initiative, with the aforementioned AfD effect almost reaching statistical significance for compliance with Corona regulations in the first survey.

4.8   Interpersonal Trust and Conspiracy Mentality

While we have analyzed attitudes towards our democratic system and the political convictions of the respondents in the previous analyses, we now want to examine aspects of individual disposition to a greater extent. While we analyzed trust in institutions, the ability of politics to solve problems, etc. above, interpersonal trust is of interest at the individual level. If it is assumed that a social crisis like the pandemic can only be solved together, then trust that not only I, but also other people will keep their promises and adhere to rules, should be an important factor in the willingness to adhere to the rules oneself. In the past, it has already been shown that interpersonal trust is associated with a reduced willingness to engage in delinquency (e.g. Austrin and Boever 1977). We therefore expect that reduced interpersonal trust will be associated with an increased willingness to act on one's own initiative in the context of the Corona crisis (see also Charron et al. 2022; Durante et al. 2021).[9] To measure interpersonal trust, we used the German short scale for measuring interpersonal trust (KUSIV3, Beierlein et al. 2012), which allows for a reliable and valid measurement of the construct with only three items.

---

[9] In contrast, Jäckle et al. (2022) found a significantly negative effect of social trust on the acceptance of Corona measures in Germany for a non-representative sample of the population. The authors argue that people with a pronounced social trust may consider Corona measures to be unnecessary because they assume that their fellow human beings would behave cooperatively without state intervention. Jørgensen et al. (2021) also report such a negative effect.

We also investigated another individual disposition, the inclination towards conspiracy beliefs. Early on, so-called Corona deniers introduced narratives into the discourse that have their roots in so-called conspiracy theories. For example, it was said that the Corona crisis had been declared in order to enable the elites to pursue their interests and impose their will on the population. The vaccinations were either attributed to the economic interests of the pharmaceutical industry or even associated with the alleged attempt to gain control over humanity through implanted technical devices (microchips). We therefore assume that the willingness to believe such conspiracy narratives should go hand in hand with Corona self-empowerment. To test this relationship, we used a questionnaire that measures so-called conspiracy mentality. By conspiracy mentality we mean the individual willingness to believe that significant events are due to the intentional activity of malicious elites who have the power to carry out the suspected conspiratorial act (Imhoff and Bruder 2014). The literature contains a questionnaire, the Conspiracy Mentality Questionnaire (CMQ, Bruder et al. 2013), which makes it possible to capture this individual willingness or disposition. We used this questionnaire, consisting of only 5 items, in our surveys.

Empirically, it turns out that conspiracy mentality indeed has the expected effect: The more people adhere to conspiracy beliefs, the more likely they are to exhibit Corona self-empowerment. The effect is considerable: Based on the values in Equation 19 in Table 4.7, under otherwise equal conditions, there is a difference between people who do not tend towards conspiracy mentality at all and those who reach the maximum value for this variable of almost one point on our self-empowerment scale.

Although the coefficient for interpersonal trust shows the expected direction, it just misses statistical significance in the model for both points in time ($p = 0.058$). However, at least for the separate evaluation of the second survey during

Table 4.7 The influence of interpersonal trust and conspiracy mentality on Corona self-empowerment		(19) Both surveys	(20) Survey 1	(21) Survey 2
	Interpersonal trust	−0.117 (0.062)	−0.011 (0.085)	−0.217* (0.091)
	Conspiracy mentality	0.102*** (0.025)	0.101** (0.034)	0.108** (0.038)

*Note: The regression coefficients of the variables of interest in this section are given. The models on which the coefficients are based include all the variables discussed in the text. Standard errors in parentheses. $*p < 0.05; **p < 0.01; ***p < 0.001.*

winter 2020/21, it reaches significance. Thus, at least for the winter 2020/21, we can argue that people who have a higher interpersonal trust tend to be less prone to Corona self-empowerment than others.

A look at the individual elements of the Corona measures shows that conspiracy mentality and interpersonal trust are particularly explanatory when it comes to the willingness to be vaccinated and the willingness to use the Corona warning app, while they make no significant explanatory contribution to compliance with the Corona rules. noteworthy differences in the separate investigation of both surveys fall on interpersonal trust. The corresponding coefficient becomes significant in a separate analysis of the second survey—regardless of the inclusion of the acceptance of self-empowerment. Both coefficients also just miss statistical significance when investigating the willingness to be vaccinated in the first survey, that is true for interpersonal trust also for the analysis of the use of the Corona app—this could, similar to the trust in science and public service broadcasting, be interpreted as an indication of the still low salience of the issue in public at this time. Finally, the conspiracy mentality makes no explanatory contribution to the use of the Corona app in the second survey and interpersonal trust just barely loses its significant influence on the willingness to be vaccinated (p = 0.052).

4.9   Attitude Towards Self-Empowerment

Finally, in this section we also look at the connection between the idea that one must always adhere to laws and Corona self-empowerment. Here we expect that people who say that one must always adhere to laws will also abide by the Corona measures. Of course, this primarily applies to complying with the Corona restrictions, while people who think that one must always adhere to laws may not necessarily have felt bound by the mere recommendation to download the Corona warning app or to be vaccinated (especially since no vaccine was available at the time of both surveys).

The variable that measures whether respondents think that one must always adhere to laws (or whether one may follow one's conscience in exceptional situations, even if this means disregarding laws), which we interpret as an indicator of the acceptance of self-empowerment, just fails to reach the significance threshold (p = 0.067) (Table 4.8).[10] If we only look at the self-reported compliance with the Corona rules, the idea that one must always adhere to laws plays a

---

[10] Since the inclusion of this variable in the regressions leads to a significant number of cases being lost, the coefficients for the remaining variables in this chapter were reported for models without inclusion of this variable. Therefore, the coefficients of the variable for

Table 4.8 The influence of the attitude towards self-empowerment on Corona self-empowerment

	(22) Both surveys	(23) Survey 1	(24) Survey 2
Follow one's conscience in exceptional situations	0.198 (0.108)	0.198 (0.108)	0.057 (0.166)

Note: The regression coefficients of the variables of interest in this section are reproduced. The regression coefficient for the acceptance of self-empowerment comes from another estimation than the coefficients in the tables above. The models on which the coefficients are based include all the variables discussed in the text. Standard errors in parentheses.

highly significant role, however. As expected, people who think that one may violate laws in exceptional situations report a higher willingness to Corona-related self-empowerment. This finding is overall very stable.

4.10   Summary

How can the diverse and nuanced results of this chapter be summarized? A first interesting finding is that Corona self-empowerment is not a *knowledge* issue. Neither formal education nor the subjective perception of one's own insight into political problems nor the objectively measured knowledge about the political system play a role in explaining. So it is probably not knowledge, but rather the *information source* that is trusted, that is important for how citizens behave towards the measures to contain the pandemic. Those who trust public broadcasters behave in accordance with the rules, in particular with regard to willingness to be vaccinated and the warning app; those who consider information from social media to be credible, on the other hand, do not adhere to the rules.

Furthermore, it is striking that *self-interest* seems to play a certain role. For example, if someone considers an infection to be likely, they are more likely to protect themselves from it through vaccination and the app. The fact that older people consistently show significantly higher compliance with rules in all surveys and in all areas of measures can also be explained by self-interest in the face of the higher risk of severe course of the disease (although of course socialization effects could also be relevant). Finally, one could also interpret the finding that people whose economic situation has worsened as a result of the

---

the acceptance of self-empowerment and the remaining variables in the tables of this chapter cannot be compared directly, as they come from different regressions.

pandemic are more likely to be vaccinated accordingly: Perhaps these people hope to contribute to overcoming the pandemic through vaccination, which could improve their economic situation.

Tightly linked to self-interest is also the finding that *deterrence* works to some extent. Of course, this only applies to the areas where there are commands and prohibitions, not to simple recommendations, such as using the app and getting a vaccination. But for compliance with the Corona restrictions, we find, on the one hand, a negative relationship between the probability of being caught and self-empowerment: Respondents who are afraid of being caught, stick to the rules more! On the other hand, the relationship for the consequences of being caught is even more robust: People who find it bad to be caught—and that seems to correlate quite well with the severity of the punishment—respects the rules more. Moreover, people who believe that one must always adhere to the law in general also abide by the Corona measures.

This relationship between fear of being caught or punished and compliance with the rules can also explain another consistent finding: namely, that if we find relationships between characteristics and pandemic-related self-empowerment, these usually occur more strongly in the question of app usage and willingness to be vaccinated. Here, it seems that violating the social norm is more clearly driven by one's own conviction, since considerations regarding possible sanctions play less of a role in the decision to act unilaterally.

Apparently more consistent than self-interest, however, is the *recognition of the need to comply*. At any rate, the strongest effect is found in our main model for the idea that the restriction of basic rights in order to protect against the pandemic is justified, and this effects remains highly significant in all robustness tests. Those who answer this question affirmatively are significantly more likely to comply with the restrictions and are more willing to be vaccinated and to install the app. Although less than three percent of those surveyed in our first poll believe that one should only obey laws if one agrees with them (see Chap. 3), empirically it appears that it is apparently at least easier to obey rules that one considers justified. Our finding that satisfaction with Corona policy is the only policy area that is consistently associated with Corona compliance also supports this statement. Finally, the finding that political interest is negatively correlated with Corona self-empowerment could also be interpreted to mean that political interest is associated with a certain understanding of the need for Corona measures, which in turn contributes to higher compliance.

However, it does not seem to be only the specific assessment of Corona policy and the associated restrictions that influence the inclination to self-empowerment in this area. Rather, we find a multitude of indications that self-empowerment in

Corona also manifests itself as a general dissatisfaction or *alienation* from the political process and democracy in Germany. This is shown, among other things, by the fact that satisfaction with democracy is itself positively associated with compliance with Corona restrictions, which means nothing other than that the people who empower themselves in relation to these rules are not only dissatisfied with the individual measures and possibly also with the incumbent government, but also with the functioning of democracy as such. The fact that both democratic and rule of law trust are negatively associated with self-empowerment—especially when the fear of infection, which ensures compliance, is low—further underlines this finding. The thesis that self-empowerment in Corona manifests a general alienation from the political system receives additional support from the finding that the election of the protest party AfD and the intention not to vote at all are positively associated with self-empowerment. The—albeit not consistently verifiable—finding that a lack of political self-efficacy in the sense of the perception of being unable to influence political decisions is correlated with the inclination to self-empowerment speaks for the alienation thesis.

And the results for the individual, psychological dispositions also support the interpretation that people who act on their own authority and do not adhere to the rules in the context of the Corona crisis show a clear alienation from the political and social system. Conspiracy mentality is a feature that includes a deep-seated mistrust of political and social institutions and their representatives. It therefore fits well with the other findings that increased conspiracy mentality, even when controlling for all other forms of mistrust in the institutions, is associated with increased readiness to act on one's own authority. A worrying observation that we have also made in our surveys is that the level of conspiracy mentality has increased significantly during the Corona pandemic ($p < .001$, $d = .26$) (Kirsch 2022; see Fig. 4.2, left). This increase is not due to an increase in the extreme level of conspiracy mentality, but to a shift in the entire distribution towards higher levels of conspiracy mentality (Fig. 4.2, right). Such an increase in mistrust could of course also lead to a general change in the social atmosphere and to an alienation of people from each other, which could also be reflected in a decrease in interpersonal trust over the course of the pandemic. We have indeed found a significant, albeit very small, decrease ($d = .098$), and this change in the social atmosphere could also have led to a significant effect of interpersonal trust on Corona self-empowerment in the second survey.

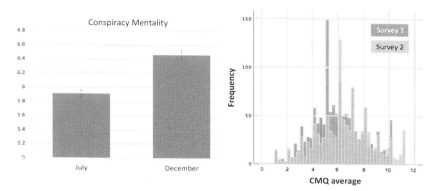

Fig. 4.2 Increase in conspiracy mentality from July to December 2020, shown as an increase in the mean (left) and as a shift in the distribution of CMQ means towards higher levels (right). (Source: own survey, own evaluation. Right part from Kirsch 2022)

References

Ackermann, Kathrin, and Reimut Zohlnhöfer. 2021. Playing by the rules – Individual and contextual determinants of abiding by the laws. Paper prepared for the (Virtual) International Conference of Europeanists 2021.

Altiparmakis, Argyrios, Abel Bojar, Sylvain Brouard, Martial Foucault, Hanspeter Kriesi, and Richard Nadeau. 2021. Pandemic politics: policy evaluations of government responses to COVID-19. *West European Politics* 44 (5–6): 1159–1179.

Anderson, Christopher J. 2022. Citizens and the state during crisis: Public authority, private behaviour and the Covid-19 pandemic in France. *European Journal of Political Research* online first, https://doi.org/10.1111/1475-6765.12524.

Austrin, Harvey R, and Patricia M. Boever. 1977. Interpersonal Trust and Severity of Delinquent Behavior. *Psychological Reports* 40(3_suppl): 1075–1078.

Bargain, Oliver, and Ulugbek Aminjonov. 2020. Trust and compliance to public health policies in times of COVID-19. *Journal of Public Economics* 192.

Behnke, Nathalie 2020. Föderalismus in der (Corona-)Krise? Föderale Funktionen, Kompetenzen und Entscheidungsprozesse. *Aus Politik und Zeitgeschichte* 70 (35-37): 9–15.

Beierlein, Constanze, Christoph J. Kemper, Anastassiya Kovaleva, and Beatrice Rammstedt. 2012. Kurzskala zur Messung des zwischenmenschlichen Vertrauens: Die Kurzskala Interpersonales Vertrauen (KUSIV3). *GESIS Working Papers* (22), available at https://www.gesis.org/fileadmin/upload/forschung/publikationen/gesis_reihen/gesis_arbeitsberichte/WorkingPapers_2012-22.pdf (last accessed: 20.06.2022).

Bruder, Martin, Peter Haffke, Nick Neave, Nina Nouripanah, and Roland Imhoff. 2013. Measuring Individual Differences in Generic Beliefs in Conspiracy Theories Across Cultures:

Conspiracy Mentality Questionnaire. *Frontiers in Psychology*, 4, available at: https://doi. org/10.3389/fpsyg.2013.00225.

Charron, Nicolas, Victor Lapuente, and Andrés Rodríguez-Pose. 2022. Uncooperative society, uncooperative politics or both? Trust, polarization, populism and COVID-19 deaths across European regions. *European Journal of Political Research* online first, https://doi. org/10.1111/1475-6765.12529.

Citrin, Jack, and Laura Stoker. 2018. Political Trust in a Cynical Age. *Annual Review of Political Science* 21: 49–70.

Dalton, Russell. 2004. *Democratic challenges, democratic choices: The erosion of political support in advanced industrial democracies.* Oxford: Oxford University Press.

Dalton, Russell. 2015. *The Good Citizen: How a Younger Generation Is Reshaping American Politics.* Washington: CQ Press.

Devine, Daniel, Jennifer Gaskell, Will Jennings and Gerry Stoker. 2020. Trust and the Coronavirus Pandemic: What are the Consequences of and for Trust? An Early Review of the Literature. *Political Studies Review* 19 (2): 274–285.

Durante, Ruben, Luigi Guiso, and Giorgio Gulino. 2021. Asocial capital: Civic culture and social distancing during COVID-19. *Journal of Public Economics* 194.

Engler, Fabian, and Reimut Zohlnhöfer. i. E. Wettbewerb um Wählerstimmen, Klimakrise und die Corona-Pandemie. Parteienwettbewerb und Regierungshandeln in der 19. Wahlperiode, in: Reimut Zohlnhöfer, and Fabian Engler (eds.). *Das Ende der Merkel-Jahre. Eine Bilanz der Regierung Merkel, 2018–2021.* Wiesbaden: Springer.

Erhardt, Julian, Markus Freitag, Maximilian Filsinger, and Steffen Wamsler. 2021. The Emotional Foundations of Political Support: How Fear and Anger Affect Trust in the Government in Times of the Covid-19 Pandemic. *Swiss Political Science Review* 27 (2): 339–352.

Grande, Edgar, Swen Hutter, Sophia Hunger, and Eylem Kanol. 2021. *Alles Covidioten? Politische Potenziale des Corona-Protests in Deutschland.* Wissenschaftszentrum Berlin für Sozialforschung: Discussion Paper ZZ 2021–601, available at https://bibliothek.wzb.eu/pdf/2021/zz21-601.pdf.

Imhoff, Roland, and Martin Bruder. 2014. Speaking (Un-)Truth to Power: Conspiracy Mentality as a Generalised Political Attitude. *European Journal of Personality* 28(1): 25–43.

Jäckle, Sebastian, Eva-Maria Trüdinger, Achim Hildebrandt, and Uwe Wagschal. 2022. A Matter of Trust: How Political and Social Trust Relate to the Acceptance of Covid-19 Policies in Germany, *German Politics* online first https://doi.org/10.1080/09644008.2021. 2021510.

Jensen, Carsten, and Reimut Zohlnhöfer. 2020. Policy knowledge among 'elite citizens'. *European Policy Analysis* 6 (1): 10–22.

Jørgensen, Frederik, Alexander Bor, and Michael Bang Petersen. 2021. Compliance without fear: Individual-level protective behaviour during the first wave of the COVID-19 pandemic. *British Journal of Health Psychology* 26 (2): 679–696.

Kestilä-Kekkonen, Elina, Aki Koivula, and Aino Tiihonen. 2022. When trust is not enough. A longitudinal analysis of political trust and political competence during the first wave of the COVID-19 pandemic in Finland. *European Political Science Review* online first, doi: https://doi.org/10.1017/S1755773922000224.

Kirsch, Peter. 2022. Selbstermächtigung and Verschwörungsglaube in den Zeiten der Pandemie. Wenn die Realität die Forschungsfrage überholt. *Forum Marsilius-Kolleg* 20: 124–130.

Marien, Sofie, and Marc Hooghe. 2011. Does political trust matter? An empirical investigation into the relation between political trust and support for law compliance. *European Journal of Political Research* 50: 267–291.

Norris, Pippa (eds.). 1999. *Critical citizens: global support for democratic government.* New York: Oxford University Press.

Person, Christian, Nathalie Behnke, and Till Jürgens. i. E. Föderale Koordination im Stresstest – zur Rolle der Ministerpräsidentenkonferenz im Pandemie-Management, in: Reimut Zohlnhöfer, and Fabian Engler (eds.). *Das Ende der Merkel-Jahre. Eine Bilanz der Regierung Merkel, 2018–2021.* Wiesbaden: Springer.

Seyd, Ben, and Feifei Bu. 2022. Perceived risk crowds out trust? Trust and public compliance with coronavirus restrictions over the course of the pandemic. *European Political Science Review* 14 (2): 155–170.

Six, Frédérique, Steven de Vadder, Monika Glavina, Koen Verhoest, and Koen Pepermans. 2021. What drives compliance with COVID-19 measures over time? Explaining changing impacts with Goal Framing Theory. *Regulation and Governance* online first, doi:https://doi.org/10.1111/rego.12440

van Rooij, Benjamin, Anne Leonore de Bruijn, Chris Reinders Folmer, Emmeke Kooistra, Malouke Esra Kuiper, Megan Brownlee, Elke Olthuis, and Adam Fine. 2020. *Compliance with COVID-19 Mitigation Measures in the United States.* Amsterdam: Amsterdam Law School Legal Studies Research Paper No. 2020–21. Available at https://doi.org/10.2139/ssrn.3582626.

Vasilopoulos, Pavlos, Haley McAvay, Sylvain Brouard, and Martial Foucault. 2022. Emotions, governmental trust and support for the restriction of civil liberties during the covid-19 pandemic. European Journal of Political Research online first, https://doi.org/10.1111/1475-6765.12513.

Fridays for Future Self-empowerment

5

5.1 Data and Method

This chapter is about the respondents' attitudes towards the Fridays for Future protests. For this purpose, we use the index described in Chap. 3 which describes the extent of agreement with the Fridays for Future protests. The variable can take the values 0 (no support), 1 (slight support), 2 (rather support) or 3 (full support) (cf. Fig. 3.6). Since this is not an interval-scaled but an ordinal-scaled dependent variable, the evaluation is carried out by means of an ordinal logistic regression.[1]

With regard to the predictor variables, we use a very similar set of variables as in the analysis of the Corona self-empowerment, but we exclude the variable block from the analysis that refers to the specific affectedness of the respondents by the Corona pandemic. Since we did not ask for an immediate individual impact of the climate crisis on the individual respondents—a shortcoming that could possibly be remedied in future surveys, for example, against the background of the floods that occurred in summer 2021 in North Rhine-Westphalia and Rhineland-Palatinate—we cannot include this aspect in the models for the attitudes towards the Fridays for Future protests. However, it is also not possible to include the

---

[1] The implementation of an ordinal logistic regression requires the proportionality assumption (English "proportional odds assumption"), which assumes that the proportion of observations in each level of the dependent variable is consistent across each level of the predictor variable. This assumption is checked by means of a chi-square test, which is very liberal and actually always rejects this assumption for large models with many, even parametric predictors and extensive samples (O'Conell 2006; Brant 1990). This is also the case for the models calculated here. However, due to the good model fit, the high variance explained and the extremely plausible results, we have decided to present and interpret the results of the models anyway. However, it should be noted that caution should be exercised when interpreting.

© The Author(s), under exclusive license to Springer Fachmedien Wiesbaden GmbH, part of Springer Nature 2023
P. Kirsch et al., *Societal Self-empowerment in Germany*,
https://doi.org/10.1007/978-3-658-40865-7_5

question of affectedness in the sense of whether the respondents themselves took part in the protests, since this question is part of the items that form our criterion variable.

First, we look at socio-economic variables, such as age, gender, education and employment status, as in the analysis of the Corona measures. In addition, this block controls for the place of residence in West or East Germany.

As in the previous analyses, we also check here whether trust in different political institutions, in parties, science, public broadcasters and social media is significant for the level of support for Fridays for Future activities. The role of satisfaction with the functioning of democracy in Germany and the response to the question of whether respondents believe that members of parliament try to keep their election promises are also taken into account in these models. In contrast to the analysis of the measures taken in the context of the coronavirus pandemic, however, the question of trust in the judiciary regarding the legality of the coronovirus measures is not included in the present analysis.

The variable block which we summarized under the term "self-efficacy" in the previous chapter, comprising the questions about the individual's ability to influence political decisions and knowledge about the most important political problems and the political system, was also included in the analysis again.

The variable block on respondents' satisfaction with the ability of German politics to solve problems was also used to explain approval of Fridays for Future protests. As in the previous chapter, the six areas of refugees, pensions, dealing with threats to Germany's security, the coronavirus pandemic, climate protection and the euro crisis are considered.

With regard to political parties, we have also examined the influence of a preference for a party on attitudes towards Fridays for Future activities. We calculated two models, one in which the parties were included in which the topics of climate change and Fridays for Future form an important part of their political agenda (Raisch and Zohlnhöfer 2020), namely the Greens, the SPD and the Left, and one model with the parties in which climate policy is less in the foreground (CDU/CSU, FDP) or which even deny climate change (AfD). This model also included non-voters and voters of other parties.

In this analysis, we also examined the influence of conspiracy mentality and interpersonal trust as personal dispositions. Finally, we also included the respondents' acceptance of self-empowering behaviour.

As in the analysis of compliance with and support for the coronavirus measures, separate models were calculated, in one of which acceptance of self-empowerment was included and in the other not. 2299 respondents were included in the models without self-empowerment acceptance (model 1 and model 3), 2039 in the models with self-empowerment acceptance (model 2 and model 4).

Since it is not to be expected that the attitudes towards Fridays for Future activities will change substantially over the course of the half year between our first and our second survey, since in the period of pandemic there were no activities of the movement at all, we have dispensed with the calculation of two separate models for the two survey points in time and have only included the time of the survey as a covariate in the model. In none of the models calculated the time of the survey explained the attitudes towards the Fridays for Future protests to a significant extent.

Overall, all four models (the two party preference models, each with and without a self-empowerment index) have a good model fit (all $\chi^2(33) > 688$). The variance explained (Pseudo-R-Quadrat according to Nagelkerke) is 32% for the two models including preferences for climate-critical parties and 30% for the models including preferences for the other parties.

The results of the analyses are presented separately below according to the blocks of variables described above.

5.2   Socio-economic Factors

For socio-economic factors, we expect age to have an influence, as it does for the Corona measures. As described above, increasing age is anyway associated with an increase in compliance with rules due to socialization (Dalton 2004, 2015; Norris 1999). In addition, it is of course to be expected that in a protest movement initiated mainly by young people and expressed in school strikes, young people are more likely to agree. There should also be greater support for the Fridays for Future movement in terms of education. On the one hand, the well-educated are more "critical citizens", whose willingness to break rules is significantly above average (Ackermann and Zohlnhöfer 2021). On the other hand, the complex relationships between human behavior and climate change, and its still limited but potentially unavoidable consequences, could become more apparent to people with increasing education. For all other variables, we have no specific theoretical expectations.

Empirically, only age shows a significant effect for the socio-economic variables (Table 5.1). As expected, the probability of agreeing with the Fridays for Future protests decreases with age. While the lack of significance for the variables on employment, unemployment/short-time work, gender and place of residence in the old or new federal states is in line with expectations, the lack of a significant

relationship between education and support for Fridays for Future is surprising—
even the sign of the coefficient contradicts our expectations. One reason for this
finding could be that the support of Fridays for Future, as seen, is particularly
high among young people such as pupils or students. However, due to their young
age, these people could (still) not have reached the higher formal education categories, even if they are on their way there. For example, pupils have not yet
formally completed their school education and therefore belong to the lowest
education category. Another reason for the surprising result could be the coding
of the education variable, which values a completed vocational training as the
second highest educational level—that is, even above the A-levels. However, the
average support for Fridays for Future by people whose highest educational qualification is a completed vocational training is not only lower than that of people
with a university degree, but also lower than that of people with A-levels and
with a lower secondary school leaving certificate, indeed, the average support for
these people is even (albeit minimal) lower than that of people who only have a
lower secondary school leaving certificate.

Table 5.1 The influence of socio-economic factors on the approval of the Fridays for Future
protests

	Model 1*	Model 2*	Model 3*	Model 4*
Age	−0.022*** (−0.029−−0.016)	−0.023*** (−0.030−−0.017)	−0.024*** (−0.030−−0.017)	−0.024*** (−0.031−−0.018)
Gender	0.047 (−0.125−0.219)	0.023 (−0.150−0.205)	0.048 (−0.124−0.220)	0.015 (−0.167−0.197)
Bildung	−0.016 (−0.074−0.041)	−0.039 (−0.010−0.022)	−0.024 (−0.082−0.034)	−0.046 (−0.107−0.015)
Beschäftigung	−0.047 (−0.227−0.133)	−0.099 (−0.289−0.092)	−0.044 (−0.224−0.136)	−0.089 (−0.279−0.101)
Unemployed or in short-time work	−0.094 (−0.429−0.241)	−0.068 (−0.433−0.297)	−0.087 (−0.424−0.249)	−0.058 (−0.425−0.309)
West Germany	0.210 (−0.032−0.451)	0.228 (−0.028−0.483)	0.189 (−0.050−0.429)	0.222 (−0.031−0.476)

*Note: The estimates (in parentheses the 95% confidence intervals) of the logarithmic ratios for
the four calculated models with all the variables discussed in the text are given. *** $p < 0.001$,
Significance level calculated with the Wald test*
*Model 1: Model with climate-critical parties, Model 2: Model with climate-critical parties and
self-empowerment acceptance, Model 3: Model with less climate-critical parties, Model 4: Model
with less climate-critical parties and self-empowerment acceptance*

5.3   Trust in Institutions and Actors

We expect to find a significant effect of trust in institutions and actors on the variable block of trust in science, as the justification for the Fridays for Future actions is based primarily on the findings of climate research. So anyone who distrusts the findings of science, which practically emphasize the man-made nature of climate change, should be skeptical of Fridays for Future. Conversely, skeptics of climate change, who should also reject school strikes, try to discredit this research. In addition, we expect a significant effect of trust in public service media on support for Fridays for Future, as their reporting has frequently addressed the issue of climate change and the scientific findings for some time.

In addition, we assume that the support for Fridays for Future is the greater the stronger the trust of the respondents in political institutions and actors is pronounced. After all, the Fridays for Future protests have a concrete political-contentual goal, namely the implementation of measures that are designed to significantly limit global warming. If this goal is to be achieved by political protest, i.e. an influence on the democratic process, it is logical to assume that the participants in the climate strike (as well as people who support this means of political influence) trust in the functioning of the political process. However, no uniform effects are to be expected for all the items examined. For example, trust in political parties may have suffered because, from the perspective of supporters of the Fridays for Future movement, they have so far done too little to combat climate change. In contrast, trust in the willingness to implement election promises should be positively related to support for Fridays for Future—because only if parties usually keep their promises from the perspective of supporters of Fridays for Future would any concessions to the demonstrators be worth anything.

Although the expected effect of trust in science is empirically shown, it shows only a very small effect (Table 5.2). People who trust science more are also more likely to agree with the protests of the Friday for Future movement. However, this effect is only significant in the models without control for the acceptance of self-empowerment. If this variable is added to the models, the relationship loses its significant explanatory value.

In addition, we also find the expected effect of the influence of trust in public service media on approval of Fridays for Future protests, but only in one of the four models, in which self-empowerment acceptance and preference for parties that have climate change less on the agenda are also controlled. Here we find greater approval among people who have more trust in public service media. However, this effect is obviously not robust.

Table 5.2 The influence of trust in institutions and actors on the approval of the Fridays for Future protests

	Model 1*	Model 2*	Model 3*	Model 4*
Trust in parliament	−0.031	−0.033	−0.029	−0.033
	(−0.075–0.013)	(−0.079–0.013)	(−0.063–0.015)	(−0.078–0.013)
Trust in state government	−0.014	−0.008	−0.016	−0.005
	(−0.055–0.027)	(−0.051–0.034)	(−0.057–0.025)	(−0.048–0.037)
Parties trust each other	−0.015	−0.017	−0.010	−0.010
	(−0.045–0.016)	(−0.049–0.016)	(−0.041–0.022)	(−0.043–0.023)
Politicians try to keep promises	0.027*	0.032*	0.023	0.029*
	(0.000–0.053)	(0.005–0.060)	(−0.003–0.050)	(0.001–0.056)
Democracy Satisfaction	−0.004	−0.003	−0.003	−0.002
	(−0.009–0.002)	(−0.009–0.003)	(−0.009–0.002)	(−0.008–0.004)
Trust in Federal Constitutional Court	−0.022	0.016	0.018	0.014
	(−0.005–0.049)	(−0.012–0.045)	(−0.009–0.045)	(−0.014–0.042)
Trust in science	0.037**	0.024	0.037**	0.023
	(0.010–0.064)	(−0.005–0.052)	(0.010–0.064)	(−0.006–0.051)
Trust in public broadcasting	0.012	0.023*	0.013	0.023
	(−0.009–0.041)	(0.000–0.046)	(−0.009–0.034)	(0.000–0.046)
Trust in social media	0.013***	0.012**	0.013***	0.012**
	(−0.006–0.020)	(−0.004–0.020)	(−0.006–0.021)	(−0.005–0.020)

*Note: The estimates (in parentheses the 95% confidence intervals) of the logarithmized ratios for the four calculated models with all variables discussed in the text are given. * p < 0.05; ** p < 0.01; *** p < 0.001, Significance level calculated with the Wald test*
*Model 1: Model with climate-critical parties, Model 2: Model with climate-critical parties and self-empowerment acceptance, Model 3: Model with less climate-critical parties, Model 4: Model with less climate-critical parties and self-empowerment acceptance

That trust in social media has a positive effect on approval of the Fridays for Future protests is unexpected. According to the statistical models, the respondents are more likely to agree with the protests, the more they trust social media. It is possible that this is due to the fact that protest movements like Fridays for Future are organized to a large extent via social networks and use social media to spread their convictions. This interpretation is also supported by the finding that we found a similar effect of social media on (non-)compliance with the Corona rules, although the results for the two areas of self-empowerment we examined differ considerably. However, it is obvious that very different information is obtained by the persons who empower themselves in the field of Corona and support Fridays for Future from social media and to which they trust.

Most of the coefficients for trust in political institutions and actors remain insignificant. As already discussed above, this is not surprising for trust in parties. The fact that trust in the Federal Constitutional Court does not have an expected influence on support for Fridays for Future is also not surprising, since the strategy for bringing about political change underlying the climate strikes does not aim at the political process, but at the judiciary. The fact that political institutions in the narrower sense play no role is probably also due to the fact that we could not include trust in the German Bundestag and the German government in the model due to the pronounced multicollinearity (cf. Chap. 4) and that state parliaments and state governments are not central climate policy actors and do not (or can not) position themselves uniformly. Therefore, the absence of a significant effect is also not surprising here. In contrast, the expected significant positive influence of the assumption that politicians try to keep their election promises on the acceptance of Friday for Future activities is found. However, it should be noted that the corresponding coefficient is only significant in three of the four models, while in model 3 the predictor just misses the significance threshold ($p = 0.083$).

5.4 Self-efficacy

In this variable block, we have summarized the variables that reflect both, interest, knowledge and insight into political relations as well as the conviction of having influence on political decision-making processes. While we were able to make the clear prediction for Corona self-empowerment that higher self-efficacy goes hand in hand with less self-empowerment, in the context of the Fridays for Future protests, we expect the opposite relationships. People who believe that they have insight into the most important political problems and who have a certain level of knowledge about the political system could also be better informed than the average citizen that science urgently calls for action to combat climate change. From this knowledge, sympathy for the Fridays for Future movement could arise, which could lead to a positive relationship between subjective or objective political knowledge and support for climate strikes.

Such a relationship should be even clearer for political interest. Politically interested people should be well informed about the public warnings of a climate crisis; at the same time, comparative research points to the fact that politically interested people are "critical citizens" and, as such, also accept breaking rules (Ackermann and Zohlnhöfer 2021).

In contrast, citizens who believe that they have no influence on the government's actions should be more reserved towards Fridays for Future. Even if such people agree with the goals of the movement, they should hardly have participated in corresponding demonstrations—simply because they do not believe that this serves the goal of climate protection, because they assume that the government is not responsive.

Interesting enough, only for political interest the expected significant positive effect can be found empirically (Table 5.3). This means that with increasing self-reported political interest, the probability of agreeing with the Fridays for Future protests increases. It is also in line with our expectations that the coefficient for the perception of lacking influence on government action is insignificant. That objective political knowledge does not seem to have any coincidental influence on support for climate school strikes could be due to the chosen indicator, which is aimed at knowledge about the institutional system (second vote), which does not necessarily have to go hand in hand with substantive knowledge about climate protection policy. The fact that the statistical model finally also shows no relationship between subjective insight into political problems and support for the Fridays for Future movement can have various reasons. Perhaps this question is also too unspecific, as it does not explicitly ask about climate problems.

5.5   Problem-solving Ability of the Political System

The analysis of the perception of the problem-solving ability of politics is also carried out for the Fridays for Future protests on the basis of the central current issues of German politics in recent years. Of course, we expect above all that the support for the Fridays for Future protests can be explained by the assessment of the problem-solving ability in the field of climate change. The central starting point of the Fridays for Future movement is precisely the perceived failure of the government to fight climate change more decisively. In this respect, the support for the climate school strikes should go hand in hand with a significant dissatisfaction with the climate policy of the federal government, so we expect a significant negative effect of the perceived problem-solving ability in the field of climate policy and the support of Fridays for Future. For the other policy areas, the theoretical expectations are less clear. On the one hand, the climate strike could be interpreted as a sign of general dissatisfaction with the performance of the political system—then we would expect significant negative

Table 5.3 The influence of self-efficacy aspects on the approval of the Fridays for Future protests

	Model 1*	Model 2*	Model 3*	Model 4*
Political Interest	0.010*** (0.006–0.015)	0.011*** (0.006–0.015)	0.010*** (0.006–0.014)	0.011*** (0.006–0.015)
No influence on government	−0.019 (−0.025–0.006)	−0.011 (−0.027–0.005)	−0.008 (−0.023–0.008)	−0.010 (−0.026–0.006)
Insight into political problems	−0.016 (−0.039–0.007)	−0.013 (−0.037–0.011)	−0.014 (−0.037–0.009)	−0.011 (−0.036–0.013)
Political knowledge	0.103 (−0.071–0.277)	−0.055 (−0.128–0.239)	0.107 (−0.068–0.282)	0.1065 (−0.119–0.249)

Note: The estimates (in parentheses the 95% confidence intervals) of the logarithmized ratios for the four calculated models with all the variables discussed in the text are given. *** p < 0.001, Significance level calculated with the Wald test
*Model 1: Model with climate-critical parties, Model 2: Model with climate-critical parties and self-empowerment acceptance, Model 3: Model with less climate-critical parties, Model 4: Model with less climate-critical parties and self-empowerment acceptance

relationships. On the other hand, however, the issue-related form of protest with a clearly defined political goal could also lead to a general trust in the system's ability to solve problems. Then the demands of the protesters would have to be understood as an invitation to the parties in power to focus more in the future their attemps to solve political problems, which they generally can, on the climate policy. Then we would expect positive relationships between satisfaction with the problem-solving ability in other policy areas and the support of Fridays for Future.

The results confirm our expectations regarding the dissatisfaction of the supporters of Fridays for Future with climate policy clearly (Table 5.4). The less the respondents were satisfied with the policy for solving the climate crisis, the more they supported the Fridays for Future protests. Here we see the highest odds ratios so far, i.e. the strongest influence of one factor on the support for the climate protests.

In addition, however—in contrast to the results for self-empowerment in the case of Corona—there are clear influences of satisfaction with the problem-solving ability in other problem areas on the support for the school strikes, but here with the opposite sign. For both refugee policy and the handling of the threat to the security of the country as well as the handling of the Corona pandemic,

Table 5.4 The influence of the assessment of the problem-solving ability of the political system on the approval of the Fridays for Future protests

	Model 1*	Model 2*	Model 3*	Model 4*
Refugee policy	0.059***	0.056***	0.059***	0.055***
	(0.038–0.081)	(0.034–0.078)	(0.038–0.080)	(0.033–0.077)
Social security for the elderly	−0.002	0.000	0.001	0.005
	(−0.025–0.021)	(−0.024–0.024)	(−0.022–0.024)	(−0.019–0.029)
Threats to Germany's security	0.035**	0.039**	0.034**	0.037**
	(0.011–0.058)	(0.014–0.064)	(0.011–0.58)	(0.012–0.062)
Corona pandemic	0.035**	0.027**	0.045***	0.037**
	(0.012–0.058)	(0.002–0.052)	(0.021–0.068)	(0.012–0.062)
Climate change	−0.114***	−0.108***	−0.126***	−0.119***
	(−0.137–−0.091)	(−0.133–−0.084)	(−0.149–−0.102)	(−0.143–−0.094)
Euro crisis	0.011	0.009	0.014	0.010
	(−0.014–0.036)	(−0.017–0.035)	(−0.011–0.039)	(−0.016–0.036)

Note: The estimates (in parentheses the 95% confidence intervals) of the logarithms of the ratios for the four calculated models with all the variables discussed in the text are given. ** $p < 0.01$; *** $p < 0.001$. Significance level calculated with the Wald test
*Model 1: Model with climate-critical parties, Model 2: Model with climate-critical parties and self-empowerment acceptance, Model 3: Model with less climate-critical parties, Model 4: Model with less climate-critical parties and self-empowerment acceptance

a positive relationship can be observed. This means that the more satisfied the respondents were with the political action in these areas, the more they supported the protests of the Fridays for Future movement. Even if no relationships can be observed in the field of social security in old age and the Euro crisis, the result can be interpreted as reflecting that the supporters of self-empowerment in the context of Fridays for Future generally assume that politics is indeed capable of solving problems, but this is not explicitly the case in the field of climate change.

5.6   Party Preferences

For the analysis of how far party preferences explain approval of the climate strikes, one can make clear predictions. In particular, the Greens are seen by voters as particularly competent in environmental and climate policy and the party has always strongly advocated for climate protection in its programmes. It is also particularly interesting to analyse the reactions of the individual parties represented in the Bundestag to the Fridays for Future protests. An evaluation of the Twitter communication of MPs from all parties represented in the Bundestag shows that the MPs from the Greens, the Left, but also the SPD have expressed themselves favourably about the protests, emphasised their legitimacy and competence and even called for participation (Raisch and Zohlnhöfer 2020). Accordingly, we assume that the supporters of the more left-wing parties should support the protests more. In contrast, we expect the supporters of the other parties represented in the Bundestag, who have expressed themselves more restrained regarding the climate strikes in Twitter communication, to reject them more. It is also to be expected that the non-voters will rather reject the protests. However, we do not make a prediction for the voters of parties not represented in the Bundestag, as these are people with a very diverse spectrum of political views.

The empirical results confirm the theoretical predictions throughout and the explanatory value of party preference represents by far the largest effect (Table 5.5). As expected, supporters of the Greens, the Left and, to a lesser extent, the SPD have a much higher probability of being positive about the climate strikes. On the other hand, supporters of the AfD, the CDU/CSU and, to a lesser extent, the FDP as well as non-voters have a much higher probability of rejecting the Fridays for Future protests. However, the respondents who are close to a party not represented in the Bundestag also tend to reject the climate protests.

Table 5.5 The influence of party preferences on the approval of Fridays for Future protests

	Model 1*	Model 2*	Model 3*	Model 4*
Alliance 90/The Greens	1.324*** (1.084–1.564)	1.312*** (1.084–1.564)		
The Left	1.064*** (0.770–1.358)	0.969*** (0.661–1.276)		
SPD	0.455*** (0.194–0.716)	0.441** (0.166–0.715)		
FDP			−0.545** (−0.938−−0.153)	−0.608** (−1.011−−0.205)
CDU/CSU			−1.052*** (−1.209−−0.835)	−1.044*** (−1.271−−0.817)
AfD			−1.092*** (−1.449−−0.736)	−1.159*** (−1.533−−0.784)
Other party			−0.397** (−0.736−−0.058)	−0.324 (−0.686–0.039)
Non-voters			−1.037*** (−1.334−−0.741)	−1.020*** (−1.346−−0.693)

Note: The estimates (in parentheses the 95% confidence intervals) of the logarithmic ratios for the four calculated models with all the variables discussed in the text are given. ** $p < 0.01$; *** $p < 0.001$, *Significance level calculated with the Wald test*
*Model 1: Model with climate-critical parties, Model 2: Model with climate-critical parties and self-empowerment acceptance, Model 3: Model with less climate-critical parties, Model 4: Model with less climate-critical parties and self-empowerment acceptance

5.7   Interpersonal Trust and Conspiracy Mentality

Our personality dispositions also came into play in the analyses of the climate protests. However, we cannot make any predictions as to whether and in which direction these will influence approval of the school strikes. While it could be argued that narratives of economic elites who prevent effective action on climate change could resonate with supporters of the protests; on the other hand, it could also be argued that it is not to be expected that people who claim to receive and take into account scientific knowledge would also be receptive to conspiracy ideas.

In fact, there is no effect of conspiracy mentality in any of the models, and thus it has no explanatory value for approval of the Fridays for Future protests (Table 5.6). In contrast, there is a significant effect of interpersonal trust in all

Table 5.6 The influence of interpersonal trust and conspiracy mentality on the approval of the Fridays for Future protests

	Model 1*	Model 2*	Model 3*	Model 4*
Interpersonal trust	0.160** (0.044–0.276)	0.132* (0.008–0.255)	0.161** (0.045–0.278)	0.138* (0.014–0.262)
Conspiracy mentality	0.010 (−0.036–0.057)	−0.001 (−0.051–0.049)	0.011 (−0.036–0.058)	0.001 (−0.050–0.051)

*Note: The estimates (in parentheses the 95% confidence intervals) of the logarithms of the ratios for the four calculated models with all the variables discussed in the text are given. * p <0.05; ** p <0.01, Significance level calculated with the Wald test*
*Model 1: Model with climate-critical parties, Model 2: Model with climate-critical parties and self-empowerment acceptance, Model 3: Model with less climate-critical parties, Model 4: Model with less climate-critical parties and self-empowerment acceptance

models. As trust in others increases, so does the likelihood of approving of the Fridays for Future protests. This relationship could be interpreted as reflecting that interpersonal trust is an expression of a prosocial orientation, characterized by good social integration, solidarity, and low fear of others. If one takes climate change as something that threatens humanity as a whole or our social life together, it is only natural that people with a prosocial orientation would support the FFF self-empowerment.

5.8 Attitude towards Self-empowerment

Finally, we report the effect of the attitude towards self-empowerment. Here, respondents were asked whether they believe that one always has to obey the law or whether there are situations in which one can act against the law for conscience' sake. Given that at least the central instrument of the Fridays for Future movement, the school strikes, represents a violation of the law, we expect that people who agree with this statement will be more likely to support the climate strikes. We can test this assumption in models 2 and 4 (Table 5.7). In both models, there is a significant effect in the expected direction. Thus, people who think that one always has to obey the law tend to disapprove of the Fridays for Future protests—presumably because they disapprove of the violation of the school attendance obligation. For example, more than 78% of those who thought that one always had to obey the law also thought that the school attendance obligation took precedence over the climate protests. Conversely, people who

Table 5.7 The influence of the attitude towards self-empowerment on the approval of the Fridays for Future protests

	Model 1*	Model 2*	Model 3*	Model 4*
Attitude towards self-empowerment	Not included in the analyses	0.306** (0.105–0.507)	Not included in the analyses	0.318** (0.116–0.520)

Note: The estimates (in parentheses the 95% confidence intervals) of the logarithmic ratios for the four calculated models with all the variables discussed in the text are given. ** p < 0.01, significance level calculated with the Wald test
*Model 1: Model with climate-critical parties, Model 2: Model with climate-critical parties and self-empowerment acceptance, Model 3: Model with less climate-critical parties, Model 4: Model with less climate-critical parties and self-empowerment acceptance

also think it justified to violate the law in exceptional cases tend to support the climate protests.

5.9   Summary

Summarizing the findings of the individual variable blocks, we find a quite consistent picture. People who are more in agreement with self-empowerment in the context of the Fridays for Future school strikes are younger, trust science more, but are also more willing to trust political actors, their fellow human beings, social media, and are generally satisfied with the performance of politics in solving problems—with the exception of the climate crisis. They are particularly close to the parties of the left spectrum, have a greater interest in politics and accept that in exceptional situations laws are broken—and they are apparently of the opinion that the climate crisis justifies such an exception. Overall, the picture emerges of "critical citizens" who do indeed believe in the changeability of politics within the system and whose consent or participation in self-empowerment in the context of school strikes results from the expectation of being able to bring about changes in political decisions and not having to change the political system. This also fits well with the appeals and attempts at dialogue of the protagonists of the Fridays for Future movement with and to politicians.

References

Ackermann, Kathrin, and Reimut Zohlnhöfer. 2021. *Playing by the rules – Individual and contextual determinants of abiding by the laws.* Paper for the 27. International Conference of Europeanists 21.–25.06.2021.

Brant, Rollin 1990. Assessing proportionality in the proportional odds model for ordinal logistic regression. *Biometrics* 46(4): 1171–1178.

Dalton, Russell. 2004. *Democratic challenges, democratic choices: The erosion of political support in advanced industrial democracies.* Oxford: Oxford University Press.

Dalton, Russell. 2015. *The Good Citizen: How a Younger Generation Is Reshaping American Politics.* Washington: CQ Press.

Norris, Pippa (ed.). 1999. *Critical citizens: global support for democratic government.* New York: Oxford University Press.

O'Connell, Ann A. 2006. *Logistic regression models for ordinal response variables.* Thousand Oaks: Sage.

Raisch, Judith, and Reimut Zohlnhöfer. 2020. Beeinflussen Klima-Schulstreiks die politische Agenda? Eine Analyse der Twitterkommunikation von Bundestagsabgeordneten. *Zeitschrift für Parlamentsfragen* 51(3): 667–682.

Discussion: Between Representational Gap and Conspiracy Belief

6.1   Instrumental vs. Expressive Self-empowerment

The results of our statistical analysis show that the people who participated in or supported the Fridays for Future protests differ significantly from those who oppose the German government's Corona strategy—a finding that was already apparent descriptively in Chap. 3 when we found a negative statistical correlation between self-empowerment in the area of Corona and in the area of Fridays for Future and when we found that none of our approximately 2,400 respondents could be classified as self-empowered in both areas.

However, our statistical results go far beyond this descriptive finding, as they enable us to work out certain characteristics of people who tend to self-empowerment in one or the other area. It should be emphasized, however, that these are, of course, "average" characteristics, so that by no means all people who support Fridays for Future or who position themselves against the government strategy in the area of Corona have to exhibit these characteristics.

We have found that people who support and possibly participate in climate school strikes can be considered politically and socially well integrated. They are young, politically interested, they trust in science and social media, but they also trust that politicians try to keep their election promises. They are satisfied with the problem-solving ability of the political system - with the important exception of climate protection policy, which may be one reason why they tend to lean more to parties to the left of the center. In addition, they have a high level of trust in their fellow human beings. In contrast, there are practically no indications that these people could be alienated from politics: neither is the perception of their own political self-efficacy low, nor are there any indications of dissatisfaction with the functioning of democracy or the election of protest or

© The Author(s), under exclusive license to Springer Fachmedien Wiesbaden GmbH, part of Springer Nature 2023
P. Kirsch et al., *Societal Self-empowerment in Germany*,
https://doi.org/10.1007/978-3-658-40865-7_6

anti-system parties. This results in a very consistent picture of people who are well integrated into the political system and believe in its problem-solving ability in principle, even if they apparently see a clear need for catch-up in the case of climate protection policy. But apparently these people believe that the system is responsive enough to also respond to the climate problem, with unconventional non-institutionalized political participation in the form of climate school strikes apparently considered appropriate, in line with an above-average acceptance of self-empowerment. Therefore, the support of Fridays for Future can be interpreted as an attempt to use school strikes to bring more political attention to the climate issue. This interpretation is supported by the findings of the study by Priska Daphi and co-authors (2021: 14–15), according to which more than half of the participants in Fridays for Future demonstrations believe that they can influence politics with their actions—a high proportion compared to participants in other demonstrations.

Conversely, people who reject the German Corona strategy seem to be largely alienated from the political system. Here too, we find that older people adhere to the rules more than younger people, and that Corona critics and supporters of FFF alike trust the social media—but the respondents probably had very different sources of information in mind here. In addition, the Corona skeptics are not only dissatisfied with the Corona policy and consider the Corona restrictions to be unjustified, but their democratic and rule-of-law confidence is low overall. In particular, satisfaction with democracy is systematically lower than for other respondents. Hence, the skepticism towards the Corona strategy of the federal government and the states not only shows a rejection of the specific measures, which could be changed, or of the respective government, which could be voted out of office, but also an alienation from the political system as a whole (see also Schäfer and Zürn 2021). And this mistrust also extends to science and the public service media. The finding that conspiracy mentality is much more widespread among Corona skeptics and interpersonal trust is much lower than among the average of the respondents fits into this pattern of basic mistrust. Unlike the Fridays for Future protesters, who are trying to influence a specific policy, the Corona skeptics thus signal with their behavior their general alienation from the political system, while the Corona measures are more likely to be the occasion than the cause of self-empowerment.

At the same time, this means that there is not one form of self-empowerment. Rather, our findings suggest that there are (at least) two types of self-empowerment, which we should also distinguish conceptually. Therefore, we propose to differentiate between expressive and instrumental self-empowerment. *Expressive self-empowerment* is norm-deviant political behavior with which the person concerned not only expresses their dissatisfaction with certain political measures and the incumbent government, but also with the functioning of democracy and the political system as a whole. Therefore, the self-empowerment in connection with the Corona measures would be referred to as expressive self-empowerment. In contrast, we understand *instrumental self-empowerment* as norm-deviant behavior of persons who are positive towards democracy, but try to support their political goals through unconventional and non-institutionalized political participation, as we have found empirically in the case of Fridays for Future.[1]

We assume that instrumental self-empowerment is unproblematic from a democratic theory perspective. Expressing dissent and working for political change is undoubtedly part of the essence of democracy. The rule violations in these cases primarily serve to gain greater media attention for the demands—a strategy that usually also succeeds, even if one may regret it from a perspective of rule compliance. Nevertheless, it is ex definitione a matter of narrowly limited rule violations, and expressive self-empowerers do not call into question the acceptance of the political system, and often not even of the violated rule itself.

The situation is quite different with expressive self-empowerment. Its appearance is a clear warning sign for the democratic political system, because it indicates that at least those members of society who resort to expressive self-empowerment experience a considerable degree of political alienation, which they document with their rule-breaking behavior. The development of measures to reduce expressive self-empowerment is therefore an important social challenge in order to prevent a further spread of this form of protest and thus counteract a destabilization of our democratic system. However, the finding that this is an expression of political alienation is too short-sighted to develop such measures. We must clarify the causes of this alienation, which can be observed in the early 2020s, in order to counter its increase. In our opinion, the party convergence observed during the Merkel years and the resulting representation gap constitute a possible cause of political alienation and thus of the expressive

---

[1] On the basis of surveys of participants of various demonstrations in Germany between 2003 and 2020, Daphi et al. (2021) come to a similar distinction. Their 'disenchanted critics' are characterized by low political trust, low satisfaction with democracy and low self-efficacy, thus resembling our expressive self-empowered. In contrast, the so-called confident critics display high political trust, high satisfaction with democracy and a high degree of self-efficacy, quite similar to our type of instrumental self-empowerment. Daphi et al. (2021) consider participants in Fridays for Future demonstrations as an example of 'confident critics', while Corona demonstrations were not investigated by Daphi and colleagues.

self-empowerment of a part of society. Although this part of the population is relatively small according to our data, the literature attests a mobilization potential of ten to twenty percent of society (Grande et al. 2021: 8).

6.2   Party Convergence and the Representational Gap

The starting point for the following considerations is the satisfaction of the respondents with the functioning of democracy in Germany. This starting point is theoretically and conceptually plausible, because political alienation should manifest itself precisely in dissatisfaction with the democratic political system, and not just in dissatisfaction with individual political measures or the government. Relying on satisfaction with democracy is also empirically plausible in terms of our results, because we were able to show that satisfaction with democracy is associated with compliance with Corona rules, i.e. people who do not accept the Corona measures are also less satisfied with the functioning of democracy. In contrast, satisfaction with democracy is not systematically related to support for the Fridays for Future movement. Finally, the functioning of democracy is also an established social science construct, which enables us to compare and supplement our own results with findings from extant research.

We follow the thesis here that, on the part of the people who are not in agreement with the Corona rules, a so-called representational gap (Jörke and Selk 2015; Merkel 2017; Patzelt 2017) could have been reflected in the dissatisfaction with the functioning of democracy. This argument is in line with the finding of Grande et al. (2021: 15–16), that the "neglected middle" supported the Corona protests (more generally on this argument see Schäfer and Zürn 2021). As in parts of the international literature—for example, Bakker et al. (2020: 292) also speak of a comparable phenomenon of "representational gap"—this term should be used purely descriptively to name the—empirically measurable—lack of parliamentary representation of opinions that are present to a significant extent in the population. In order to speak of a representational gap, on the one hand, a convergence of the political positions of the established parties in certain, highly salient policy areas would have to be observed, and on the other hand, a divergence of the (converging) party positions and the preferences of a part of the population would neet to be found.

Was there a thus defined representational gap in salient policy fields in Germany during the Merkel years? In particular with regard to coping with the Euro crisis between 2009 and 2015, corresponding relationships can be very well traced empirically because, on the one hand, a larger number of roll call votes took place in the Bundestag on various measures to rescue the Euro, and on the other hand data from population surveys are available on the voted topics. Figure 6.1 shows the results of the votes in the Bundestag for a number of relevant measures of 2010 (EFSF), 2011 (EFSF increase), 2012 (ESM establishment and Fiscal Compact) and 2015 (3rd Greece rescue package) and compares them to the results of population surveys of the Forschungsgruppe Wahlen's Politbarometer survey.

It is striking from the data that in the Bundestag there were broad majorities for all measures that went far beyond the circle of the respective governing parties. While in the vote on participation in the EFSF in May 2010, the then opposition parties SPD and Greens at least abstained and only the Left voted against the bill, SPD and Greens supported the increase in the EFSF (September 2011), the establishment of the ESM and the Fiscal Compact (both June 2012) with few exceptions. Only the Left continued to vote unanimously against all bills. After the change of government in 2013 and the FDP's failure to win representation in the Bundestag, the voting behaviour of the parties remaining in the Bundestag did not change. Even the Greens, who remained in opposition, voted in favour of the 3rd Greece rescue package (August 2015), while the Left remained opposed. Accordingly, we find approval rates of often more than 80% and—even more importantly—rejections of less than 20% of the deputies, thus considerable convergence. In addition, an important part of the no votes came from dissidents from the coalition parties. This concerned the SPD in the case of the Fiscal Compact, and the Christian democrats in the other votes. The no votes from the Christian democrats was even the largest group of those voting against in the vote on the 3rd Greece rescue package. On the other hand, the no votes came from the Left, which voted unanimously (with the exception of the third Greece rescue package). While the dissent in the CDU/CSU was justified by the concern that the crisis countries were not consolidating their budgets enough, the Left rejected the laws because they did not want to support the austerity policy alledgedly reflected in them.

The preferences in the population were clearly distributed differently. With the exception of the Fiscal Compact, no majority can be found for any measure among the respondents. What is more, all other measures were rejected by a majority of those surveyed, often by wide margins, as was particularly the case with the increase in the EFSF, against which more than three quarters of those surveyed spoke out. In contrast, the very high approval of the Fiscal Compact with 78% of those surveyed is remarkable. The fact that the respondents apparently broadly supported stricter fiscal rules for the EU member states, as they were decided with the Fiscal Compact, suggests that the rejection of the other

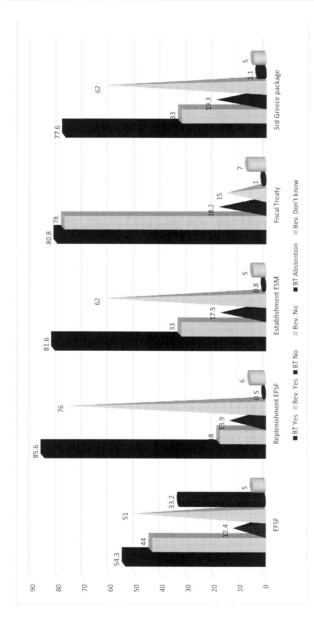

Fig. 6.1 Voting results in the Bundestag and public opinion on issues of Euro rescue. (Sources: for the voting results in the Bundestag: PlPr. 17/44, 21.05.2010, p. 4443 (EFSF); PlPr. 17/130, 29.09.2011, p. 15,236 (EFSF increase); PlPr. 17/188, 29.06.2012, p. 22,740 (ESM establishment); PlPr. 17/188, 29.06.2012, p. 22,736 (Fiscal Pact); PlPr. 18/118, 19.08.2015, p. 11,487 (3rd Greece package); for the population data: Forschungsgruppe Wahlen Politbarometer May 2010 (EFSF); September I 2011 (EFSF increase); September I 2012 (ESM establishment and Fiscal Pact); August 2015 (3rd Greece package))

rescue measures for the euro was not to be interpretedas a rejection of a European austerity policy-as was the reason for the no votes of the Left-, but rather as a rejection of a greater financial involvement of the Federal Republic in the so-called sovereign debt crisis. If this interpretation is correct, there was no party in the Bundestag for the majority of those surveyed that represented their political ideas—and this in an area of politics that was considered one of the biggest problems of German politics by the voters at the respective times.[2] The government and most of the opposition parties voted for the measures rejected by the majority of the population, the Left apparently rejected the measures for different reasons than the majority of skeptical citizens, and the remaining dissidents in the Bundestag, mainly from the ranks of the CDU/CSU parliamentary group, formed a clear minority in their party. Only in 2013 did the euro-skeptic AfD establish itself, but it was not represented in the Bundestag until 2017.

A similar pattern may also have shaped migration policy in the context of the so-called refugee crisis in 2015—although this pattern is less well supported by data because there was no vote in the Bundestag on the immigration of a large number of refugees. Nevertheless, the relevant literature makes it clear that in particular the parties represented in the Bundestag, i.e.the coalition partners CDU/CSU and SPD, but also the Left Party and the Greens, supported the course in refugee policy—albeit against the massive resistance of the-at that time still extra-parliamentary-AfD (Alexander 2017; Engler et al. 2019). At the same time, surveys by Infratest dimap's DeutschlandTrend between October 2015 and April 2016 show a majority of the population rejected this policy. In the five corresponding surveys, between 39 and 42% of those surveyed said they were satisfied or very satisfied with the German government's refugee policy, while between 57 and 60% said they were less or not satisfied with this policy (Infratest dimap 2016: 14)—namely a policy that was in turn supported by all parties represented in the Bundestag. Again, it can be concluded that the majority position of the population was probably not represented in the Bundestag. Again, this was a highly salient policy in the public eye that was always seen as the most important problem in German politics by a very large majority of those surveyed between

---

[2] According to a Politbarometer poll in May 2010, only 16% of those surveyed considered the euro crisis to be one of the two most important problems in Germany. In September 2011, this proportion had risen to 40 and 42%, in June 2012 it was at 41% and in August 2015 at 36%. Around the time of the Bundestag votes, public attention was sometimes even higher, for example in October 2011 at 63%, in July 2012 at 54% and in July 2015 at 49%. Between July 2011 and January 2013 (with the exception of the months of March and April 2012) as well as in March/April 2013 and in July 2015, and thus also in the period of the votes in question, the euro crisis even topped the list of the most important problems.

September 2014 and May 2019 (with the exception of July 2015): Between 75 and 88% of those surveyed in the Politbarometer saw migration as one of the two most important problems in Germany.

This means that we find strong convergence between the parties represented in the Bundestag on the two central challenges of the period between 2010 and 2019, the euro rescue and the refugee policy. This does not apply to the Left Party in the euro rescue policy without qualification, as it consistently voted against the relevant measures. But with the rejection of what the party perceived to be a European austerity policy, it probably did not represent the majority of skeptical citizens who were probably more afraid of a stronger financial involvement of the Federal Republic in solving the euro crisis, as the broad support for the Fiscal Compact shows.

The handling of the Corona crisis, which, as we saw in Chap. 3, was of great importance to the vast majority of German voters in 2020 and 2021, may finally have contributed to the idea of a broad programmatic agreement between the established parties. Due to the multi-level structure of German federalism, it must have been difficult for many people to determine which level and thus in many cases which party they should attribute responsibility for (alleged) policy errors to. Since all established parties seemed to be involved in the decisions—an perception that was probably further strengthenedby the increasing role of the State Prime Ministers' Conference (Behnke 2021)—and clear alternatives were difficult (if at all) to discern, the perception of programmatic convergence is likely to have increased.

Even political science experts were unable to identify any significant differences in the programmatic positioning of the established German parties in the run-up to the 2021 federal election (Jankowski et al. 2022). Over 300 experts located the German parties in relation to different policy areas. With regard to Corona policy, the parties were be placed on a scale from 1 to 20, on the one hand in relation to the tradeoff between health protection and restrictions on freedoms, with low values indicating a prioritization of health; and on the other hand in relation to the emphasis on state or individual responsibility, with low values implying that the respective party assigns an important role to the state.

The average classification of the federal parliamentary parties can be found in Fig. 6.2. Here too, a widespread agreement between the established parties is evident. With regard to the prioritization of health protection, Greens, SPD, CDU/CSU and Left differ by only 1.5 points on the 20-point scale, while the distance between these four parties is even smaller at 0.8 scale points with regard to the role of the state. While these parties consistently tended to prioritize health protection and attributed a significant role to the state, the AfD was always close

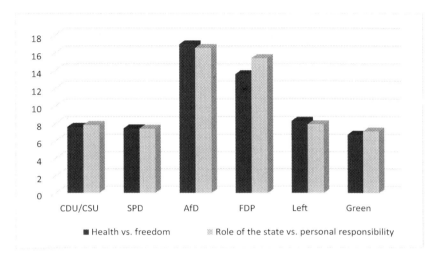

Fig. 6.2 Party positions on Corona policy. (Source: own illustration, data from Jankowski et al. 2022)

to the opposite poles of the scale and therefore far removed from the established parties. However, in the case of Corona policy, the position of the FDP is to be emphasized, which also significantly more than the other established parties prioritized the civil rights even against health protection and relied on more individual responsibility.

In contrast to the two policy areas considered so far, however, we do not find a majority rejection of policy with regard to Corona at least in our research period. On the contrary, the majority of our respondents was satisfied with the political handling of the Corona pandemic in both survey periods, although with a declining trend: In summer 2020, more than two out of three respondents (68.3%) had shown satisfaction with the measures to contain the pandemic, with eight percent undecided and 23.5% dissatisfied, while the approval in the following winter sank to 55.8% (eight percent undecided, 35.9% rejection)—but still included the majority of respondents.

Convergence across parties was also evident in other policy areas, although it was usually the CDU/CSU that abandoned its previously more conservative positions (Oppelland 2019), for example—with great support from voters—on the minimum wage and in nuclear policy (Zohlnhöfer and Engler 2015), but also in family policy, conscription and same-sex marriage, which the party did not support, but cleared the way for its adoption by declaring the vote to be a matter of conscience and thus giving up its veto power. This means that the Christian democratic parties revised their originally conservative-authoritarian social policy positions in many issue areas in the 2010s. Migration policy is certainly the most spectacular example here, but by no means the only one. The programmatic revision by the Christian Democrats was certainly due in part to certain external shocks and the need to find coalition partners in the absence of a majority with the "natural" coalition partner FDP. However, the programmatic changes could have left a "neglected middle" (Grande et al. 2021: 15–16) among voters who reacted to this change with alienation from politics and the democratic system, as we discuss in the following section.

6.3   The Representational Gap and Satisfaction with Democracy

What do these developments have to do with the satisfaction of citizens with the functioning of democracy? If one follows the recent relevant literature, the perception plays an important role, whether the programmatic positions of the established parties differ or not. While voters prefer limited but recognizable party differences, the perception of large polarization between the main parties of a party system leads to decreased satisfaction with democracy; but the perception that the parties differ not at all, weighs much heavier, by a factor of 5–6 (Ridge 2022; see also Torcal and Magalhães 2022). However, this relationship does not apply to all citizens in the same way. Rather, it is above all citizens who are not affiliated with any (established) party and who feel represented by no party, for whom the effects of party convergence on dissatisfaction with democracy are particularly prominent (Ridge 2022). Other studies underscore this finding. For example, Bakker et al. (2020) show that citizens tend to political alienation ("disaffection") when substantial-contentual representational gaps exist, that is, when there are large differences between the individual position of a citizen and the positions of the parties represented in parliament. Socio-political issues such as migration and Europe play a significant role in this context. In the German case of the 2010s, the party convergence could have led to the perception of a representational gap in particular among a part of rather conservative-authoritarian voters who, after the liberalization of the socio-political positions of the Christian democratic parties, could have felt represented by no party anymore. In contrast, the effects should hardly have occurred among rather left-liberal voters, who possibly also perceived convergence, but no representation deficit.

At the same time, recent findings also confirm the theoretically already obvious assumption that the election of anti-system parties is positively correlated with the (perceived) convergence of mainstream parties (Grant 2021; Spoon and Klüver 2019; see also Bakker et al. 2020). The rise of the AfD, obviously associated with the Euro-, but above all with the migration crisis (e.g. Engler et al. 2019: 320–321; Franzmann 2019: 339–342), impressively demonstrates this argument for the German case. There is therefore some evidence that the programmatic convergence of the established parties in the Federal Republic in many central policy areas and the shift to the left of the Christian democrats in socio-political policy in particular have led to a representational gap that could have been perceived above all by voters with socio-politically conservative-authoritarian preferences. This part of the electorate is likely to have then turned to the AfD as a protest and anti-system party or not voted at all.

However, according to the results of a recent empirical study, the choice of a protest party does not seem to be able to compensate for the increasing dissatisfaction with democracy—at least as long as the voters of this protest party have to assume that the party they have voted for has no chance of successfully feeding their positions into the political process (Hobolt et al. 2021); indeed, some studies even argue that the choice of populist parties increases dissatisfaction (Rooduijn et al. 2016). At the same time, voters who tend to parties that have never reached government are particularly dissatisfied with democracy and these people rate the responsiveness of the political system as particularly low (Anderson et al. 2005: 153)—obviously because their preferences are not taken into account by this system. Translated to the German case, this means that the satisfaction with democracy of people who vote for the AfD because they feel unrepresented by the established parties does not increase significantly even when the party they have voted for enters parliament—as long as the party remains excluded from the coalition game, which is the case in Germany with regard to the AfD.

Our survey data allow us to check these considerations at least indirectly. For this purpose, we used a linear regression with the variable measuring the satisfaction with the functioning of democracy in Germany as the dependent variable, that is, the variable to be explained. In addition to a number of control variables, namely gender, age, education, place of residence in West or East Germany, interest in politics, self-placement on the left-right scale, subjective insight into political problems, trust in politicians, conspiracy mentality and interpersonal trust as well as a control for the survey round, we included satisfaction with problem solving in six policy areas as explanatory variables.

If the argument of the representational gap is correct, we should find that on the one hand lower satisfaction with Euro rescue policy as well as refugee policy, but also with Corona policy goes hand in hand with lower satisfaction with democracy. This means that we expect a significantly positive coefficient for these variables. Of course, it is generally always the case that dissatisfaction with political decisions should have a negative effect on satisfaction with the system that makes these decisions. At the same time, however, we expect the respondents to distinguish between satisfaction with individual policies, with the government and with the democratic system. Necessarily, many political decisions do not turn out the way we want them to, but we seldom take these decisions as an opportunity to call the democratic system as a whole into question. Accordingly, satisfaction with the functioning of democracy should be affected above all by those policies that are particularly important to the respondents and where they feel particularly poorly represented. These relations should be especially true for decisions that are already slightly in the past, as in the case of Euro rescue and migration policy.

If essentially people with conservative-authoritarian preferences in social policy do not feel represented (anymore), there should also be a positive relationship between satisfaction with the way Germany deals with threats to its security and satisfaction with democracy. The policy of internal and external security is an important item for conservative-authoritarian people and could therefore well reflect the possible alienation of these people beyond highly salient crises. It would therefore be expected that conservative-authoritarians are dissatisfied with security policy and that this dissatisfaction is then also reflected in satisfaction with democracy as a whole.

If, on the other hand, Fridays for Future supporters are dissatisfied with climate policy but not with the functioning of democracy, this relationship should tend to be insignificant—satisfaction with democracy should not be tarnished by dissatisfaction with climate policy, but the conviction should prevail that democracy is responsive enough to also respond to the climate crisis.

Finally, it should be noted that our argument refers to the libertarian-authoritarian cleavage. Therefore, no or at most a weak relationship should be found between satisfaction with social security of older people (as a classical socio-economic item) and satisfaction with democracy—dissatisfaction with this topic should have less of an impact on dissatisfaction with democracy than with libertarian-authoritarian issues, because, according to our argument, there are political representatives for welfare state issues who also have a sufficiently plausible chance of being able to come to power in Germany.

The data of 2,372 respondents could be included in the regression and the variance explained is 60.2%. The control variables show the expected directions for the most part and are mostly significant (cf. Table 6.1). For example, older age, higher education and living in West Germany are associated with higher satisfaction with democracy, as are political interest, trust that politicians will keep their promises or trust in fellow human beings. Not surprisingly, increasing conspiracy mentality is associated with less satisfaction with democracy. While the coefficients for subjective insight into political problems and self-placement on the left-right scale fail to reach the significance threshold, at least the signs go in the expected direction, namely that people who see themselves politically on the left tend to be more satisfied with the functioning of democracy.

However, of greater importance for our study are the findings on the effects of satisfaction with the problem-solving ability in the different policy areas. And in fact, our expectations are confirmed overall very clearly. Hardly surprisingly, satisfaction with the Corona policy has the strongest effect, recognizable by the largest absolute value of the six coefficients. This means that people who were not satisfied with the Corona management were also less satisfied with the functioning of democracy as a whole. This is not surprising, as the surveys were conducted at a time when the Corona crisis was in the public spotlight and people were also directly affected in their everyday lives by Corona politics. That the satisfaction with this policy is also reflected in satisfaction with democracy is hardly surprising under these conditions—but of course this finding corroborates our expectations.

The next largest significant positive effect is found for coping with the Euro crisis. This result supports the argument about the representational gap, suggesting that people who were still dissatisfied with policiess to save the euro in 2020, even though the Euro crisis had already reached its (provisional) peak in 2015, were also systematically less satisfied with the functioning of democracy. The same direction is indicated by the similarly highly significant, but much smaller coefficient for satisfaction with the handling of the refugee crisis. Although it is surprising that the effect of (dis)satisfaction with migration policy is only half as large as that of satisfaction with European policy, the result as a whole does speak for the argument of the representational gap: Satisfaction (or dissatisfaction) with European and migration policy also has a systematic effect on satisfaction with democracy even years after the respective crises have subsided. This is very much in line with the theory that it is precisely those who rejected these policies but did not find effective political representatives for their position who are systematically less satisfied with the functioning of democracy.

Similarly, we also find a significantly positive relationship, which is even larger than that for the refugee crisis, for satisfaction with the way security policy threats are dealt with. This finding also suggests that the authoritarian-libertarian cleavage is particularly important for satisfaction with the functioning

Table 6.1 Determinants of satisfaction with the functioning of democracy

Constant	3.313 3.367
Age	0.066** (0.023)
Gender	−0.265 (0.693)
Education	0.955*** (0.226)
Interest in politics	0.065*** (0.016)
Insights into political problems	−0.142 (0.089)
Politicians try to keep promises	0.825*** (0.095)
Left-right	−0.133 (0.090)
First or second survey	1.982*** (0.694)
West Germany	5.094*** (0.957)
Conspiracy mentality	−1.342*** (0.178)
Interpersonal trust	1.595*** (0.463)
Refugee policy	0.331*** (0.087)
Social security for the elderly	0.179 (0.092)
Threats to Germany's security	0.618*** (0.093)
Corona pandemic	1.255*** (0.085)
Climate change	−0.150 (0.086)
Euro crisis	0.669*** (0.099)

Note: In parentheses standard error. * $p < 0.05$; ** $p < 0.01$; *** $p < 0.001$

of democracy—possibly precisely because there is a representational gap here that systematically leads to dissatisfaction among people whose political position is not represented by any established party. This is also supported by the fact that the coefficient for satisfaction with pension policy (just) fails to achieve statistical significance, so that satisfaction with welfare state issues does not seem to have a systematic effect on satisfaction with democracy. Again, this finding could be interpreted to mean that (dis)satisfaction with welfare state policy affects satisfaction with democracy to a lesser extent precisely because the positions of the political parties on the welfare state have converged to a lesser extent in 2020[3] and accordingly the dissatisfied have political alternatives with realistic chances of government participation. Alternatively, this finding could be explained by the fact that the respondents on average attach less importance to the welfare state when they assess democracy in Germany.

Finally, the coefficient for satisfaction with climate policy also fails to achieve statistical significance. This finding already confirms our expectations, but even more interesting is the sign of the coefficient, which is negative! This means that, if there is any connection at all between satisfaction with climate policy and satisfaction with democracy, this connection is negative, i.e. people are more satisfied with democracy the less satisfied they are with climate policy. Since the coefficient fails to achieve statistical significance, even if only by a slight margin ($p = 0.081$), the result should not be interpreted substantively. But nevertheless, it shows that people who are dissatisfied with climate policy are by no means necessarily dissatisfied with the functioning of democracy—quite the contrary to people who are dissatisfied with the management of the Corona crisis, the Euro rescue policy, refugee and security policy!

The results presented so far remain substantively unchanged if the respondents' voting intention is controlled for instead of their position on the left-right-scale or trust in different media is additionally included. Even when the two surveys are considered separately, the results change in only one respect. Only satisfaction with the social security of older people becomes significant in the first survey, all other results remain substantively unchanged. Even more important is another control, namely the control for the economic situation of the respondents. For this purpose, we first examined how unemployment or short-time work affects satisfaction with democracy. We find neither a direct effect of unemployment on satisfaction with democracy nor does the inclusion of this variable change the

---

[3] This is at least true for the late 2010s. In the second half of the 2000s, especially after the far-reaching Hartz labor market reforms of the second Schröder government, there may well have been a perception of an economic and social policy party convergence, which was reflected in the formation of the Left in the (West German) party system.

effect of the variables measuring satisfaction with the political ability to solve problems. In addition, we have also included the variable in the regression, which reflects the change in the economic situation of the respondents as a result of the pandemic, in addition to and instead of the unemployment variable. Since we only asked this question in the second survey, the results therefore relate solely to the situation in November/December 2020. Not surprisingly, a deterioration in one's own economic situation leads to less satisfaction with the functioning of democracy. At the same time, however, the inclusion of this variable does not affect how satisfaction with the ability of politics to solve problems in different areas affects satisfaction with democracy. Hence, dissatisfaction with Europe and refugee policy leads to dissatisfaction with the functioning of democracy in Germany, while this is not the case for dissatisfaction with climate and welfare policy, and this finding is independent of the economic situation of the respondents.

6.4　The Representational Gap from a Psychological Perspective

If one asks oneself how the phenomenon of the representational gap and its effects can be described from a psychological point of view, two, by no means mutually exclusive, aspects seem to play a role, social exclusion and the feeling of lack of control.

People who do not feel represented experience a *loss of control*. They get the impression that they have no influence on important decisions that affect their own lives. But this also means that they lose some control over these decisions. This feeling of loss of control becomes even stronger in unpredictable crises such as the Corona pandemic, because here too it is no longer possible to predict with certainty what people will expect in the near future. One way to avoid fear of loss of control is to seek simple explanations that simplify complex reality. Such explanations are called conspiracy theories.

In the psychology of conspiracy theories, the function of conspiracy myths to regain control is discussed as a key mechanism. Douglas and colleagues (2017) summarize the phenomenon under the term "epistemic motive", which is about making inexplicable events controllable by finding causal explanations. The influence of lack of control on the formation of illusory beliefs can even be shown at the level of perception. Whitson and Galinsky (2008) found that an experimentally indicated loss of control leads to an increase in illusory perception. Intriguingly, the loss of control in this study also led to an increase in conspiracy beliefs. The connection between political uncontrollability and conspiracy theories was also confirmed by a study by Kofta and colleagues (2020), which dealt with the origin of anti-Semitic conspiracy theories and showed that it was specifically the political uncontrollability and not the political uncertainty that led to an increase in anti-Semitic conspiracy myths. Furthermore, It can be shown historically that social crises characterized by sudden, hardly controllable changes also lead to an increase in conspiracy myths (van Prooijen and Douglas 2017). In turn, such conspiracy mentality correlates in our study with self-empowerment with regard to the Corona measures. Therefore, these studies suggest that the perception of a loss of control caused by the representation gap may have led to an increase in expressive self-empowerment.

For example, with regard to the meaning of *social exclusion,* it could be shown that the feeling that the basic values of society are no longer shared seems to be a driving force behind conspiracy theories (Federico et al. 2018). In addition, low social integration and an insecure attachment style as well as social exclusion increase the susceptibility to conspiracy narratives (Freeman and Bentall 2017; Koroma et al. 2022). At the same time, it was precisely during the Corona pandemic that a strong social cohesion emerged among conspiracy supporters, which satisfies the need for attachment and social inclusion and thus apparently massively reinforces the conviction of belonging to the few "enlightened" people.

In a recently published study on the relationship between political attitudes and conspiracy mentality (Imhoff et al. 2022), which examined over 100,000 respondents in 26 countries, it was shown, among other things, that conspiracy mentality is more pronounced among supporters of opposition parties than among supporters of parties involved in the government. For the manifestation of conspiracy mentality, it therefore seems to be important to what extent a person feels that his or her convictions are implemented in political decisions—which fits well with the argument from political science research that supporters of parties that do not permanently come to power are particularly dissatisfied with democracy. Even if people who feel little or not at all represented in the political system were not explicitly examined in this study, the results can therefore be interpreted as indirect support for a connection between representation gap and conspiracy mentality. Both the lack of representation and the support of a party not involved in the government entail at the individual level the feeling on the one hand to be excluded from the political processes and on the other hand (and thus related) to have no influence or control over political decisions. These findings also support our assumption that the feeling of lack of control and social exclusion seem to be the mechanisms that mediate the connection between the representation gap, conspiracy mentality and ultimately expressive self-empowerment.

Therefore, we postulate a—admittedly simplified—model of how the representation gap leads to a feeling of lack of control and social exclusion, which in turn leads to an increase in expressive self-empowerment (Fig. 6.3). An empirical test of the model, however, cannot be carried out within the scope of this book and must be left to future research. In addition, the model does not contain any statements as to how far the representational gap, the experienced loss of control or social exclusion also have an effect on societ al self-empowerment without the mediation of the conspiracy narratives. Also this question must be empirically examined in the future.

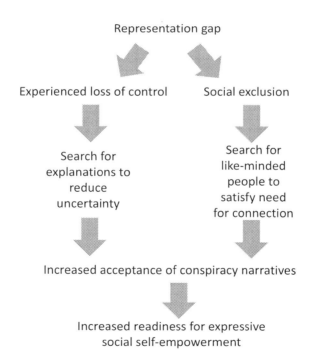

Fig. 6.3 Hypothetical model of the psychological mechanisms mediating the relationship between the representation gap and expressive self-empowerment. (Source: own representation)

6.5   Summary

From this chapter, we can conclude that there are plausible theoretical arguments and empirical findings that suggest (but do not prove!) that the causes of political estrangement from the democratic political system of the Federal Republic, which is reflected in the expressive self-empowerment of the rejection of the Corona measures, go back further than the beginning of the pandemic. Obviously, the (dis)satisfaction with the Euro rescue and the refugee policy has a lasting effect on satisfaction with democracy. Those people who were dissatisfied in areas, in which a representational gap can be plausibly explained by the significant convergence of policy positions of political parties, and who felt excluded from political decision-making processes because no party represented in the Bundestag with a realistic coalition option represented their own position, were on average also less satisfied with the functioning of democracy in Germany and thus more likely to resort to expressive self-empowerment in connection with Corona measures. Similar relationships seem to apply to security policy, and thus to a policy area that is traditionally of interest to conservative-authoritarian voters, who may have lost their representative through the liberalization of the positions of the Christian democratic parties on the authoritarian-libertarian axis. Against this background of already existing dissatisfaction with democracy, the Corona crisis may have acted as a catalyst: not only continued the satisfaction with the problem-solving ability of politics to decline, but also the feeling of political uncontrollability was added to the feeling that the personal life had become uncontrollable. Both developments then also reinforced conspiracy mentality and thus also the increasing readiness for expressive self-empowerment.

In ontrast, we do not find the slightest indications that these relationships also exist in climate policy. Dissatisfaction with climate policy is not translated into dissatisfaction with democracy, which in turn is not a predictor of instrumental self-empowerment within the Fridays for Future movement.

References

Alexander, Robin. 2017. *Die Getriebenen. Merkel und die Flüchtlingspolitik: Report aus dem Innern der Macht.* München.

Anderson, Christopher J., André Blais, Shaun Bowler, Todd Donovan, and Ola Listhaug. 2005. *Losers' Consent: Elections and Democratic Legitimacy.* Oxford: Oxford University Press.

Bakker, Ryan, Seth Jolly, and Jonathan Polk. 2020. Multidimensional incongruence, political disaffection, and support for anti-establishment parties. *Journal of European Public Policy* 27(2): 292–309.

Behnke, Nathalie. 2021. Handlungsfähigkeit des Föderalismus in der Pandemie. Überlegungen zur Kompetenzverteilung anlässlich der ‚Bundesnotbremse‘. *Recht und Politik* 57(3): 369–380.

Daphi, Priska, Sebastian Haunss, Moritz Sommer, and Simon Teune. 2021. Taking to the Streets in Germany – Disenchanted and Confident Critics in Mass Demonstrations. *German Politics*, online first DOI: https://doi.org/10.1080/09644008.2021.1998459.

Douglas, Karen M., Robbie M. Sutton, and Aleksandra Cichocka. 2017. The Psychology of Conspiracy Theories. *Current Directions in Psychological Science* 26(6): 538–542.

Engler, Fabian, Svenja Bauer-Blaschkowski, and Reimut Zohlnhöfer. 2019 Disregarding the Voters? Electoral Competition and the Merkel Government's Public Policies, 2013–17. *German Politics* 28(3): 312–331.

Federico, Christopher M., Allison L. Williams, and Joseph A. Vitriol. 2018. The role of system identity threat in conspiracy theory endorsement. *European Journal of Social Psychology* 48(7): 927–938.

Franzmann, Simon T. 2019. Extra-Parliamentary Opposition within a Transforming Political Space: The AfD and FDP under Merkel III between 2013 and 2017. *German Politics* 28(3): 332–349.

Freeman, Daniel, and Richard P. Bentall. 2017. The concomitants of conspiracy concerns. *Social Psychiatry and Psychiatric Epidemiology* 52(5): 595–604.

Grande, Edgar, Swen Hutter, Sophia Hunger, and Eylem Kanol. 2021. *Alles Covidioten? Politische Potenziale des Corona-Protests in Deutschland.* Wissenschaftszentrum Berlin für Sozialforschung: Discussion Paper ZZ 2021–601, available at https://bibliothek.wzb.eu/pdf/2021/zz21-601.pdf.

Grant, Zack P. 2021. Crisis and Convergence: How the Combination of a Weak Economy and Mainstream Party Ideological De-Polarization Fuels Anti-System Support. *Comparative Political Studies* 54(7): 1256–1291.

Hobolt, Sara B., Julian M. Hoerner, and Toni Rodon. 2021. Having a say or getting your way? Political choice and satisfaction with democracy. *European Journal of Political Research* 60 (4): 854–873.

Imhoff, Roland, Felix Zimmer, Oliver Klein, João H.C. António, Maria Babinska, Adrain Bangerter, Michal Bilewicz, Nebojša Blanuša, Kost Bovan, Rumena Bužarovska, Aleksandra Cichocka, Sylvain Delouvée, Karen M. Douglas, Asbjørn Dyrendal, Tom Etienne, Biljana Gjoneska, Sylvie Graf, Estrella Gualda, Gilad Hirschberger, … and Jan-Willem van Prooijen. 2022. Conspiracy mentality and political orientation across 26 countries. *Nature Human Behaviour*. https://doi.org/10.1038/s41562-021-01258-7.

Infratest dimap. 2016. ARD DeutschlandTREND. April 2016. Eine Studie im Auftrag der tagesthemen, available at https://www.tagesschau.de/inland/deutschlandtrend-529.pdf.

Jankowski, Michael, Anna-Sophie Kurella, Christian Stecker, Andreas Blätte, Thomas Bräuninger, Marc Debus, Jochen Müller, and Susanne Pickel. 2022. Die Positionen der Parteien zur Bundestagswahl 2021: Ergebnisse des Open Expert Surveys. *Politische Vierteljahresschrift* 63(1): 53–72.

Jörke, Dirk, and Veith Selk. 2015. Der hilflose Antipopulismus. *Leviathan* 43 (4): 484–500

Kofta, Mirosław, Wiktor Soral, and Michał Bilewicz. 2020. What breeds conspiracy anti-semitism? The role of political uncontrollability and uncertainty in the belief in Jewish conspiracy. *Journal of Personality and Social Psychology* 118(5): 900–918.

Koroma, Dennis, Maria I. Pestalozzi, and Hansjörg Znoj. 2022. How Social Exclusion, Embitterment, and Conspiracy Beliefs Mediate Individual's Intention to Vaccination against COVID-19: Results from a Moderated Serial Mediation Analysis. *Psychopathology* 55(2): 93–103.

Merkel, Wolfgang. 2017: Kosmopolitismus versus Kommunitarismus: Ein neuer Konflikt in der Demokratie, in: Philipp Harfst, Ina Kubbe, and Thomas Poguntke (eds.): *Parties, Governments and Elites. The Comparative Study of Democracy.* Wiesbaden: Springer VS, 9–23.

Oppelland, Torsten. 2019. Profilierungsdilemma einer Regierungspartei in einem fragmentierten Parteiensystem: Die CDU während der Amtszeit der Regierung Merkel III, in: Reimut Zohlnhöfer, and Thomas Saalfeld (eds.): *Zwischen Stillstand, Politikwandel und Krisenmanagement. Eine Bilanz der Regierung Merkel 2013–2017,* Wiesbaden: Springer VS, 63–85.

Patzelt, Werner J. 2017. Der 18. Deutsche Bundestag und die Repräsentationslücke. Eine kritische Bilanz. *Zeitschrift für Staats- und Europawissenschaften* 15: 245–285.

Ridge, Hannah M. 2022. Just like the others: Party differences, perception, and satisfaction with democracy. *Party Politics* 28(3): 419–430.

Rooduijn, Matthijs, Wouter van der Brug, and Sarah L. de Lange. 2016. Expressing or fuelling discontent? The relationship between populist voting and political discontent. *Electoral Studies* 43: 32–40.

Schäfer, Armin, and Michael Zürn. 2021. *Die demokratische Regression. Die politischen Ursachen des autoritären Populismus.* Berlin: Suhrkamp.

Spoon, Jae-Jae, and Heike Klüver. 2019. Party convergence and vote switching: Explaining mainstream party decline across Europe. *European Journal of Political Research* 58: 1021–1042.

Torcal, Mariano, and Pedro C. Magalhães. 2022. Ideological extremism, perceived party system polarization, and support for democracy. *European Political Science Review* 14: 188–205.

van Prooijen, Jan-Willem, and Karen M. Douglas. 2017. Conspiracy theories as part of history: The role of societal crisis situations. *Memory Studies* 10(3): 323–333.

Whitson, Jennifer A., and Adam D. Galinsky. 2008. Lacking Control Increases Illusory Pattern Perception. *Science* 322(5898): 115–117.

Zohlnhöfer, Reimut, and Fabian Engler. 2015. Politik nach Stimmungslage? Der Parteienwettbewerb und seine Policy-Implikationen in der 17. Wahlperiode, in: Reimut Zohlnhöfer, and Thomas Saalfeld (eds.): *Politik im Schatten der Krise. Eine Bilanz der Regierung Merkel, 2009–2013.* Wiesbaden: Springer, 137–167.

Conclusion: What to do Against (Expressive) Self-empowerment?

7.1   Summary of Findings

The starting point of this book—and our joint scientific deliberations—was the suspected increase in violations of rules that are justified on idealistic, political or ethical grounds—we speak of social self-empowerment. The legal discussion of the concept already pointed at the genuinely social-political dimension of the phenomenon, which can essentially be classified as civil disobedience and thus understood as an expression of political demands.

We have tried to determine the extent of social self-empowerment in two representative surveys of the population. If we use a broad definition and already talk about social self-empowerment even when people are willing to break the law in exceptional situations in order to follow their conscience, this is a mass phenomenon; almost two thirds of our respondents fall into this category. If, on the other hand, respondents are asked whether one is allowed to take the law into one's own hands or whether one must only adhere to rules if one agrees with them, if one is threatened with being caught or if the government also adheres to the rules, the agreement rapidly decreases. Our concrete examples, the climate school strikes and the Corona measures, also provide nuanced findings. But they also show that social self-empowerment by no means only affects a vanishingly small minority. For example, just under a quarter of those surveyed supported the idea of demonstrating for the climate during school time—and thus contrary to the legal obligation to attend school—and at least six percent of our respondents said that they had only adhered to the Corona restrictions to a limited extent. The phenomenon that is being considered here is thus undoubtedly relevant to society.

Our further analyses in turn confirm that social self-empowerment is a multi-layered phenomenon. This can already be read off the fact that, at least based on a

P. Kirsch et al., *Societal Self-empowerment in Germany*, https://doi.org/10.1007/978-3-658-40865-7_7

strict definition, none of the persons interviewed by us tend to self-empowerment in the field of Corona and in the field of climate at the same time. The more detailed statistical investigations underline that the persons, who tend to one or the other form of self-empowerment, display quite different characteristics and properties. The supporters of Fridays for Future are well integrated into the political system, show no pronounced tendency towards protest parties or dissatisfaction with democracy, are satisfied with the performance of the political system with the exception of climate policy, do not tend to conspiracy theories and have social trust. The people who turn against the Corona strategy of the political decision-makers in Germany, on the other hand, prove to be partly alienated from the political system: lower satisfaction with democracy, lower satisfaction with the problem-solving ability of the political system, mistrust of the public media and science, a tendency towards non-voting or the AfD as a protest party, significantly higher conspiracy belief and lower trust in the political system and other people tend to characterize these respondents.

Because of these striking differences, we suggest to call these different manifestations instrumental and expressive self-empowerment, respectively. Instrumental self-empowerment serves the political support of individual policy projects through unconventional and non-institutionalized forms of political participation. Civil disobedience is hoped to generate attention for the issue in order to put it on the political agenda and to implement the desired political solution. Basically, persons employing instrumental self-empowerment appear to be well integrated; hence this form of self-empowerment—even if one may disapprove of the breach of law—appears to be unproblematic for democracy in principle.

However, caution is advised. It is by no means guaranteed that instrumental self-empowerment does not turn around and take on detrimental forms. The climate strikes are a good example of this scenario. The supporters of Fridays-for-Future can certainly point to mobilization successes in the first phase of the movement and claim an influence on the agenda-setting of federal politics for themselves (Raisch and Zohlnhöfer 2020). Even if there are no strong indications that the German Climate Protection Act of 2019 was influenced to a substantial extent by Fridays-for-Future (Engler and Zohlnhöfer 2022), the law and its tightening in reaction to a ruling of the Federal Constitutional Court showed a development in the direction desired by the FFF supporters; and also the good opinion poll results of the Greens in the relevant period and the excellent prospects of this party, which is supported by the FFF supporters to a greater extent than average, to become part of the next federal government could have had a positive influence on the perception of the responsiveness of the political system. But what, one could ask, if a federal government with a strong green coalition partner does not achieve the climate change, even if that were only because the Russian attack war against Ukraine delays the change? It is conceivable that under such conditions there will be increasing frustration among the FFF supporters with the performance of the political system, which, if the situation persists, may be generalized and increasingly turn into expressive self-empowerment. The activists of the "last generation" in Germany or "extinction rebellion" internationally, which we were not able to investigate in this book, could be exemplary for at least partly also expressive self-empowered in the climate area. If the climate policy change does not come quickly enough for the FFF supporters, their numbers could increase significantly.

Expressive self-empowerment, on the other hand, which we tend to find for the critics of the Corona management, is likely to be problematic for democracy. Our investigations suggest that this form of societal self-empowerment represents an alienation from the democratic political system and the perception of a representation gap on the part of the relevant respondents. This assessment is underlined by the fact that Armin Schäfer and Michael Zürn (2021) find very similar connections in their analysis of authoritarian populism as we do for expressive self-empowerment. In both cases, it seems that a representation gap forms the core and starting point of the alienation from the democratic system. We have understood a deficit of representation primarily in the substantive sense, that is, with regard to the political positions of certain population groups which are hardly represented or do not have any prospect of being represented successfully.

This representation gap is accompanied by unequal descriptive representation (Schäfer and Zürn 2021: 93–96, also Fortin-Rittberger and Kröber 2021 for the 20th Bundestag), not least a massive over-representation of academics in decision-making bodies. In the 12th electoral term of the Bundestag (1990–1994), the proportion of MPs with a lower secondary school leaving certificate was still 9.4%, but then fell continuously to 1.6% in the 18th electoral term (2013–2017). At the same time, the proportion of MPs with a university degree increased in the same period from 78.0% to 86.1%, with a peak of 90.5% in the 17th electoral term (Feldkamp 2015: Section 3.9). In the 19th Bundestag (2017–2021) at the centre of this book, just under 82% of MPs had completed their university studies.[1] It at least appears plausible that different perspectives on political problems and possibly also different preferences may be associated with different levels of education, which could help to explain the substantial representation gap.

---

[1] https://www.forschung-und-lehre.de/politik/mehr-als-80-prozent-akademiker-im-bundestag-1861 (last accessed 21.06.2022).

7.2   What to do?

Finally, the question arises as to what should be done in the face of these findings. Can and should a democratic society do something about societal self-empowerment, in particular about expressive self-empowerment—and above all: What could be effective against the alienation from the democratic system expressed in expressive self-empowerment?

To the extent that self-empowering behaviour is also illegal behaviour, it might seem obvious to push back societal self-empowerment through the punishment of corresponding behaviour. Our analysis of Corona self-empowerment, in particular the compliance with Corona rules, indeed suggested that people were more likely to comply with the Corona restrictions if they considered it likely that they would be caught violating them, but above all if they found it "bad" to be caught—and there is reason to believe that the perception of being caught is related to the severity of the punishment. Shouldn't we conclude from this finding that self-empowering behaviour should decrease if the penalties are increased and the likelihood of being discovered is increased, for example by higher police presence?

However, the broader empirical literature tends to speak against the expectation that harsher penalties will have a sustainable deterrent effect (van Rooij and Fein 2021: 12–45). In addition, the administrative effort for the close monitoring and punishment of acts of social self-empowerment, as we discuss them in this book, would be disproportionate, indeed prohibitively high. And worse still: people who are alienated from the political system and do not see their political preferences represented are unlikely to be re-integrated into the political system with the help of penalties and deterrence. Rather, the opposite effect of further alienation and an even stronger feeling of social exclusion is to be expected, as the self-empowered would probably experience the political system in particular, but also the majority society in general, as even more hostile in the event of punishment.

In a similar way, one can argue against another frequently observed approach: the social exclusion of the self-empowered. This approach is also easily comprehensible at first: If people do not adhere to the rules, they no longer belong to the circle of "good democrats" and do not deserve public attention; their arguments should not be widely discussed and thus possibly made acceptable for more citizens. However, it is very doubtful whether such an approach conveys new trust in the political system and the functioning of democracy in Germany to alienated persons. It is rather to be feared that such an approach has a counterproductive effect, since the affected persons are already alienated and the conspiracy narratives are only confirmed and served by the social exclusion. In this respect, the use of such a strategy also depends on how small one considers the circle of the alienated to be. If it is a "tiny minority of those full of hate", as Federal Chancellor Olaf Scholz (2021: 335) put it in his first government declaration to the German Bundestag, this approach may appear promising because the number of those excluded is very limited. But when is the self-empowering minority so tiny that it can be excluded without further damage to the community? In Chap. 3 we identified 3.4% of the respondents as strict Corona self-empowered, which would be, extrapolated to the electorate, around 2 million voters in Germany. Is that still a tiny minority? And if the Corona self-empowered are less strictly delimited, this number becomes even larger; Grande et al. (2021) estimate the mobilization potential of the anti-Corona protests at 10% of the population, that would be over 6 million eligible voters. Can this group of people be excluded without further deepening the representation deficit and further strengthening the feeling of social exclusion?

While it cannot be denied that the democratic society clearly does not have to accept everything that the self-employed impose on it, it must be noted that the social exclusion must not affect a relevant population group. Therefore, social exclusion also appears to be an unsuitable general strategy against expressive self-empowerment.

Assuming that expressive self-empowerment is at least partially the result of political alienation and a lack of trust in democracy, a response should rather focus on regaining this political trust. However, this does not appear to be simple at all and the cautious suggestions from the literature are not all convincing. For example, in a recent review article, Citrin and Stoker (2018: 64) discuss various ways to regain political trust. One possibility would be a sustained period of successful government policy. One could think of the early phase of the Federal Republic with the "economic miracle" as an example. But in view of the succession of crises and challenges in recent times, which promise no quick solutions, such a lasting success story seems difficult to imagine. In addition, there is likely to be disagreement as to when a policy can be considered successful, particularly regarding issues discussed on the authoritarian-libertarian dimension of political competition. The admission of refugees from war-torn countries is classified by some as a humanitarian necessity and political success, while others perceive it as a political failure. The latter would then classify a reduction in the number of refugees as a success, which the first group would consider a failure. As a result, there will be few policies that are perceived by the majority of people as a success—especially in the field of social policy.

An alternative way to overcome alienation is seen by Citrin and Stoker (2018: 64) in the rise of charismatic leaders, "whose virtues and popularity would be projected onto the institutions and increase confidence in them." However, the rise of such a personality cannot be raised to a program—often such people are simply lacking or they are populist politicians who have contributed little empirically to the improvement of the democratic quality of a country (Schäfer and Zürn 2021: 167–194). But even if the charismatic personality is not a populist, it is by no means certain that her or his work actually has a positive effect on political trust. The France of Emmanuel Macron leaves room for doubt here.

To the extent that democratic estrangement is actually related to a representational gap, it appears plausible to close such a representational gap. To the extent that the representational gap is based on insufficient descriptive representation of certain population groups—not least of non-academics, but also of people with a migrant background—institutional adjustments would be conceivable. Above all, it would be necessary to question the recruitment patterns of parties (Schäfer and Zürn 2021: 211–213). In this respect, however, the constitutional guarantee of freedom of association is to be observed.

Similar problems also arise in the production of substantive representation: In democratic systems, of course, no one can prescribe to parties which policy positions they are to represent and with whom they agree or form coalitions. In this respect, the convergence of political positions can not be prevented in principle and in some of the cases described, the party positions have been largely in agreement for a long time. This is particularly true for policies regarding European integration, since all established parties have always considered European integration to be a "national interest" (Müller-Brandeck-Bocquet 2006). The actual exclusion of the AfD from government responsibility by the refusal of the other parties to form coalitions with the right-wing populists is neither unconstitutional, nor politically objectionable. Here, the parties have to make decisions and there are certainly good reasons not to form coalitions with the AfD—even if their participation in government might increase the perception among their voters that their own positions are represented.

However, on a lower level, a change in the political debate, in the media discourse and in the debates in social media would be conceivable, which could reduce the representational gap, namely the equal participation in the political discourse. If the positions expressed by expressive self-empowered women and men hardly occur in the mass media discourse or are not taken seriously and swept off the table from the outset, hardly any trust in the political institutions and the media will arise and the feeling of a loss of control will be intensified. This means first of all that the media coverage should not over-represent a certain position, least of all the position of the government, as has occasionally been claimed for the media coverage of the migration crisis (Kepplinger 2019; Wendt 2020: 413–415). If trust is to arise in the democratic process, one's own position in this process must at least be recognizable.

Secondly, this position must also be taken seriously enough. The TINA argument ("There is no alternative") prevailed not least during the Euro rescue policy—"If the euro fails, Europe fails" was how the then German Chancellor Angela Merkel (2010: 4126) put it in a nutshell. But in many other crises of recent years, the need for action has also been cited as something that politics allegedly has to follow (hence, the right populist "Alternative for Germany" (AfD) took the commitment to an alternative into its name). This argument, which was used so frequently by Margaret Thatcher that "Tina" even became her nickname (Lawson 1992: 100), is effective precisely because it portrays alternative courses of action as impractical and otherworldly and thus potentially makes representatives of alternative approaches appear incompetent. This reduces the political space for action, which is beneficial in the short term for the government, but in the medium term increases frustration at the alleged lack of alternatives. Conversely, the naming and critical discussion of alternative political options in public might also create a perception of representation among those citizens whose preferences are not then reflected in the output of the political process.

It also seems just as important that the critical discussion is open-ended and that certain positions are not discredited from the outset. Wolfgang Merkel (2021) argues that the political discourse on the migration, climate and coronavirus crises has been characterized above all by moralization and scientization.[2] But by moralization and scientization, the positions of critics of these policies would be devalued as amoral, backward-looking and simply scientifically wrong, they would be referred to as "climate" or "coronavirus deniers": "But you can't have a discourse with liars and deniers. They are first conceptually and then really socially excluded from society" (Merkel 2021: 10; our translation). This exclusion, as one can easily imagine, leads to estrangement from the political system, in which the people concerned no longer see their positions represented and in which they feel they have no influence on public opinion formation; at the same time, it leads to a turn to echo chambers in social media, where feedback with the political discourse in the rest of society is then hardly possible anymore.

---

[2] In the case of the debates in the German parliament on Corona mitigation policies, moralization on the part of the government or the media cannot be proven (Zohlnhöfer i. E.). Nonetheless, the argument is probably plausible in principle for the broader public discourse (for the debate on migration, see Wendt 2020).

If this is to be prevented, then the positions of the corresponding population groups must be considered legitimate; then they must not be characterized as impractical, immoral or stupid in advance and their representatives must not be excluded, but respected politically. This does not mean that one must respect every single position, even if it is racist or contemptuous of humanity—by no means! And it certainly does not mean that one must hold these positions to be correct and advocate their implementation. But democracy lives from the openness of results (Merkel 2021) and that also means that political opponents must respect each other as legitimate representatives in the public debate, especially when they are resolute and passionate about their respective different positions.

References

Citrin, Jack, and Laura Stoker. 2018. Political Trust in a Cynical Age. *Annual Review of Political Science* 21: 49–70.

Engler, Fabian, and Reimut Zohlnhöfer. 2022. Wettbewerb um Wählerstimmen, Klimakrise und die Corona-Pandemie. Parteienwettbewerb und Regierungshandeln in der 19. Wahlperiode, in: Reimut Zohlnhöfer, and Fabian Engler (eds.): *Das Ende der Merkel-Jahre. Eine Bilanz der Regierung Merkel 2018–2021.* Wiesbaden: Springer.

Feldkamp, Michael F. 2015: *Datenhandbuch zur Geschichte des Deutschen Bundestages.* Abrufbar unter https://www.bundestag.de/datenhandbuch (zuletzt zugegriffen am 21.06.2022).

Fortin-Rittberger, Jessica, and Corinna Kröber. 2021. Der neu gewählte Deutsche Bundestag. Ein Schritt in Richtung eines „repräsentativen" Parlaments? *Aus Politik und Zeitgeschichte* 47–49: 34–40

Grande, Edgar, Swen Hutter, Sophia Hunger, and Eylem Kanol. 2021. *Alles Covidioten? Politische Potenziale des Corona-Protests in Deutschland.* Wissenschaftszentrum Berlin für Sozialforschung: Discussion Paper ZZ 2021–601, abrufbar unter https://bibliothek.wzb.eu/pdf/2021/zz21-601.pdf.

Kepplinger, Hans Mathias. 2019. Die Mediatisierung der Migrationspolitik und Angela Merkels Entscheidungspraxis, in: Reimut Zohlnhöfer, and Thomas Saalfeld (eds.): *Zwischen Stillstand, Politikwandel und Krisenmanagement. Eine Bilanz der Regierung Merkel 2013–2017.* Wiesbaden: Springer VS, 195–217.

Lawson, Nigel. 1992. *The View from No. 11. Memoirs of a Tory Radical.* London u. a.: Bantam Press.

Merkel, Angela. 2010. Regierungserklärung durch die Bundeskanzlerin zu den Maßnahmen zur Stabilisierung des Euro, in: *Plenarprotokolle des Deutschen Bundestages,* 17. Wahlperiode, 42. Sitzung, 19. Mai 2010, pp. 4125–4131.

Merkel, Wolfgang. 2021. Neue Krisen. Wissenschaft, Moralisierung und die Demokratie im 21. Jahrhundert. *Aus Politik und Zeitgeschichte* 28–29/2021: 4–11

Müller-Brandeck-Bocquet, Gisela. 2006. Europapolitik als Staatsraison, in: Manfred G. Schmidt, and Reimut Zohlnhöfer (eds.): *Regieren in der Bundesrepublik Deutschland. Innen- und Außenpolitik seit 1949.* Wiesbaden: Verlag für Sozialwissenschaften, 467–490.

Raisch, Judith, and Reimut Zohlnhöfer. 2020. Beeinflussen Klima-Schulstreiks die politische Agenda? Eine Analyse der Twitterkommunikation von Bundestagsabgeordneten. *Zeitschrift für Parlamentsfragen* 51(3): 667–682.

Schäfer, Armin, and Michael Zürn. 2021. *Die demokratische Regression. Die politischen Ursachen des autoritären Populismus.* Berlin: Suhrkamp.

Scholz, Olaf. 2021. Regierungserklärung, in: *Plenarprotokolle des Deutschen Bundestages,* 20. Wahlperiode, 8. Sitzung, 15. Dezember 2021, pp. 333–349.

Van Rooij, Benjamin, and Adam Fine. 2021. *The Behavioral Code. The Hidden Ways the Law Makes us Better ... or Worse.* Boston: Beacon Press.

Wendt, Fabian. 2020. Moralismus in der Migrationsdebatte, in: Christian Neuhäuser, and Christian Seidel (eds.): *Kritik des Moralismus.* Berlin: Suhrkamp, 406–421.

Zohlnhöfer, Reimut. i. E. Moralisierung im deutschen Bundestag? Das Beispiel der Corona-Politik, in: Ekkehard Felder, Friederike Nüssel, and Jale Tosun (eds.): *Moral und Moralisierung,* Berlin: de Gruyter.

Appendix 1: Questionnaire Design, Representativeness of Respondents and Variable Coding

The results presented in this book are to a large extent based on two surveys that we carried out as part of our project "Societal Self-Empowerment: Extent, Reasons, Consequences, Measures" at the Marsilius-Kolleg of Heidelberg University. The Marsilius-Kolleg is also to be warmly thanked for financially supporting the surveys.

The surveys were carried out by the Bamberg Centre for Empirical Studies (BACES). They are both web-based interviews of Access Panelists of the provider respondi AG, with a quota of panelists according to the characteristics of gender, age (5 classes) and education (3 classes). The first survey was in the field from 30.06. to 07.07.2020, 1351 people were interviewed. In the second survey, 1099 people were interviewed from 30.11. to 11.12.2020.

Questionnaire Design

The questionnaire contains some standard questions, the formulation of which was partly taken over from the German Longitudinal Election Study (GLES), the Role of Government surveys of the International Social Survey Programme, as well as the Mannheim Corona Study (Blom et al. 2020) in order to ensure comparability with other studies. Furthermore, established questionnaires were used, in particular the short scale for measuring interpersonal trust (KUSIV3, Beierlein et al. 2012), the Conspiracy Mentality Questionnaire (CMQ, Bruder et al. 2013) and the Big-Five Inventory (Rammstedt et al. 2014). Other questions were formulated by the authors, some of which were inspired by the study by van

© The Editor(s) (if applicable) and The Author(s), under exclusive license to Springer Fachmedien Wiesbaden GmbH, part of Springer Nature 2023
P. Kirsch et al., *Societal Self-empowerment in Germany*,
https://doi.org/10.1007/978-3-658-40865-7

Rooij et al. (2020). Individual questions were only asked in the first or second survey. Appendix 2 contains the complete set of questions.

Representativeness

In the following, we discuss the representativeness of the two surveys based on selected variables. Table A.1 shows that the data of our surveys on the gender distribution are relatively close to the data of the representative election statistics for the German federal election 2021. In contrast, for both surveys in comparison to the representative election statistics, there is an under-representation of people who are older than 60 years—which is not surprising in an online survey. With regard to the place of residence in East or West Germany or Berlin, the distribution in our survey corresponds quite closely to the population distribution according to the official data of the Federal Statistical Office. When comparing the distribution of the highest educational degree, the categories asked in our survey differ somewhat from those of the Federal Statistical Office. Where the categories are comparable, however, there is a relatively large agreement—with the exception of people without a school leaving certificate, who are particularly under-represented in our first survey. Finally, we compare the distribution of party preferences with data from the Sunday question of the ARD-DeutschlandTrend by Infratest dimap. For this purpose, we have always used the data that were closest to the periods of our surveys. Here, for the first survey, there is a certain under-representation of supporters of the government parties in our data with an over-representation of the opposition, in particular the Left. This pattern weakens in the second survey, here, on the other hand, voters of the Greens are somewhat less represented in our data than in the Infratest survey, while, above all, the share of voters of other parties is slightly higher in our data than in the DeutschlandTrend data. However, it should be kept in mind that, of course, the DeutschlandTrend itself is based on surveys that are subject to a fluctuation range of 2 to 3 percentage points and thus do not necessarily reflect the "true" political mood to the nearest percentage point. Overall, however, there is a high representativeness of our survey data.

Variable Coding

Not all items on the questionnaire could be used directly for statistical analysis. We explain below how the calculation was carried out for the relevant variables.

Table A.1 Representativeness of the surveys

	1. Survey		2. Survey	
Gender		Calculated according to Federal Election Director 2022b: 8		Calculated according to Federal Election Director 2022b: 8
Female	49.95	51.5	50.2	51.5
Male	49.95	48.5	49.6	48.5
Diverse	0.1	*	0.2	*
Age		Federal Election Commissioner 2022a: 2		Federal Election Commissioner 2022a: 2
18–29	20.2	14	20.6	14
30–59	61.6	47	60.6	47
60 and more	18.2	39	18.8	39
East/West Germany		Calculated according to Statistisches Bundesamt 2021 (as of 31.12.20)		Calculated according to Statistisches Bundesamt 2021 (as of 31.12.20)
East Germany	15.7	15.0	13.1	15.0
West Germany	79.5	80.6	82.6	80.6
Berlin	4.8	4.4	4.3	4.4
Formation		Calculated according to Federal Statistical Office 2020: 21 (As of 2019)		Calculated according to Federal Statistical Office 2020: 21 (As of 2019)
Without school leaving certificate	0.4	4.0	1.7	4.0
Secondary school diploma	29.5	28.6	28.4	28.6
High school and college	35.5	33.5	35.9	33.5
Party preferences		Infratest dimap 2022: Sunday question 02.07.20		Infratest dimap 2022: Sunday question 11.12.20
CDU/CSU	29.8	37	32.2	36
SPD	12.2	16	15	16
AfD	13.1	10	11.7	9

(continued)

Table A.1 (continued)

	1. Survey		2. Survey	
FDP	6.0	5	5.3	6
Linke	11.2	7	9.1	7
Grüne	20.1	20	17.4	20
Other	7.5	5	9.3	6

* People of diverse genders are not shown separately in the representative election statistics due to the small number, but are added to the male respondents

Dependent variables

Corona self-empowerment: This variable aggregates the variables for self-assessment of compliance with the rules, the willingness to use the Corona Warning App, the willingness to be vaccinated and the participation in anti-Corona demonstrations. All variables were recoded so that higher values indicate a higher degree of self-empowerment. When asked about compliance with the Corona rules, the answer "Always followed the rules" was coded with 0, "mostly" with 1, "often" with 2, "sometimes" with 3, "rarely" with 4 and "never" with 5. For the Corona Warning App, the following answers were coded with 0: The app has already been installed, is very likely to be installed, and cannot be installed for technical reasons; 1 is awarded for the answer, installation of the app is "somewhat likely", 2 for "rather unlikely" and 3 for "very unlikely". When asked about the willingness to be vaccinated, the answer "very likely" was rated 0, "rather likely" 1, "partly-partly" 2, "unlikely" 3 and "not at all likely" 4. Since only a dichotomous answer option exists for the question of participation in demonstrations, 0 is coded for non-participation and 2 for participation in the demonstrations. The so-coded variables were added up. In total, the aggregation results in a value range between 0 (= always kept to the Corona restrictions, warning app installed, very likely vaccination, no participation in demonstrations) and 14 (never followed the rules, installation of the app and vaccination very unlikely, participation in demonstrations against Corona restrictions).

Fridays for Future self-empowerment: This variable aggregates the variables for approval of the climate school strikes, participation in the strikes and the assessment that the demonstrations took place during school time. For each question, we coded the answer option with 1, which expresses support for the FFF school strikes (school strikes are correct, own participation, participation of a family member, support for demonstrations during school time), while all other answer options were coded with 0. Subsequently, the three recoded items were added up.

Independent variables

Unemployed and short-time work: Respondents who answered the question about current employment with "currently unemployed" or "currently in short-time work" were assigned a 1, all other respondents a 0.

Employees: Respondents who stated in the question about current employment that they were employed full-time or part-time were assigned a 1, all other respondents a 0.

Democratic trust: sum of the variables for trust in the Bundestag, in the federal government, in the parties and in the state government as well as democracy satisfaction. Democracy satisfaction was calibrated in such a way that its value range corresponds to that of the other variables.

Attitude towards self-empowerment: The answer "I can't say" to the question of whether one must always obey the law or whether one may follow one's conscience in exceptional situations was coded as missing, so that the respondents concerned were not taken into account in analyses with this variable.

Interpersonal trust: sum of the three items of the short scale for measuring interpersonal trust (KUSIV3, Beierlein et al., 2012).

East/West Germany: respondents who stated that they lived in the federal states of Brandenburg, Mecklenburg-Western Pomerania, Saxony, Saxony-Anhalt and Thuringia were assigned the value 1, respondents who stated that they lived in another federal state were assigned the value 2.

Party vote: From the item on the party that the respondents would vote for in the next federal election, dummy variables were coded for each party represented in the Bundestag, for other parties and for non-voters, with 1 being assigned if a person indicated the corresponding party, and 0 otherwise.

Political knowledge: In the question of which vote would be decisive for the distribution of seats in the Bundestag election, the correct answer ("the second vote") was coded with 1, all other answers with 0.

Rule of law trust: sum of the variables for trust in the Federal Constitutional Court and for trust that "the courts will effectively protect the rights of citizens against the far-reaching measures to contain the Corona pandemic".

Social media: For this variable, the answers to the trust in "Youtube", "Blogs on the Internet" and "Social Media (Facebook, Twitter, Instagram etc.)" were added up.

Conspiracy mentality: mean of the five items of the Conspiracy Mentality Questionnaire (CMQ, Bruder et al. 2013).

Probability of infection: The question of the probability of infection with the Corona virus was only asked to those persons who were not already infected or had an infected family member; therefore, these persons were originally coded as missing. In these cases, we assigned a value of 22, which is above the maximum value of 21 that was assigned to persons who believed that it was "absolutely probable" that they or a family member would become infected.

References

Beierlein, Constanze, Christoph J. Kemper, Anastassiya Kovaleva, and Beatrice Rammstedt. 2012. Short Scale for Measuring Interpersonal Trust: The Short Scale Interpersonal Trust (KUSIV3). *GESIS Working Papers* (22), available at https://www.gesis.org/fileadmin/upl oad/forschung/publikationen/gesis_reihen/gesis_arbeitsberichte/WorkingPapers_2012-22.pdf (last accessed: 20.06.2022)

Blom, Annelies G., Carina Cornesse, Sabine Friedel, Ulrich Krieger, Marina Fikel, Tobias Rettig, Alexander Wenz, Sebastian Juhl, Roni Lehrer, Katja Möhring, Elias Naumann, and Maximiliane Reifenscheid. 2020. High Frequency and High Quality Survey Data Collection. *Survey Research Methods* 14(2): 171–178.

Bruder, Martin, Peter Haffke, Nick Neave, Nina Nouripanah, and Roland Imhoff. 2013. Measuring Individual Differences in Generic Beliefs in Conspiracy Theories Across Cultures: Conspiracy Mentality Questionnaire. *Frontiers in Psychology, 4*, available at: https://doi.org/10.3389/fpsyg.2013.00225.

Bundeswahlleiter. 2022a. *Short Report on the Results of the Representative Election Statistics for the Federal Election 2021*, available at https://www.bundeswahlleiter.de/dam/jcr/610da2d6-54e8-429b-9d9c-83c41aebe42d/btw21_rws_kurzbericht.pdf (last accessed on 13.06.2022a).

Bundeswahlleiter. 2022b. *Election to the 20th German Bundestag on 26 September 2021. Issue 4 Voting Participation and Voting by Gender and Age Groups*, available at https://www.bundeswahlleiter.de/dam/jcr/8ad0ca1f-a037-48f8-b9f4-b599dd380f02/btw21_heft4.pdf (last accessed on 13.06.2022b).

Infratest dimap. 2022. *Sonntagsfrage Bundestagswahl*, available at https://www.infratest-dimap.de/umfragen-analysen/bundesweit/sonntagsfrage/ (last accessed on 13.06.2022).

Rammstedt, Beatrice, Christoph J. Kemper, Mira Céline Klein, Constanze Beierlein, and Anastassiya Kovaleva. 2014. *Big Five Inventory (BFI-10). Zusammenstellung sozialwissenschaftlicher Items und Skalen (ZIS)*, available at https://doi.org/10.6102/zis76.

Statistical Federal Office. 2020. *Educational level of the population. Results of the Microcensus 2019*, available at https://www.destatis.de/DE/Themen/Gesellschaft-Umwelt/Bildung-Forschung-Kultur/Bildungsstand/Publikationen/Downloads-Bildungsstand/bildun gsstand-bevoelkerung-5210002197004.pdf?__blob=publicationFile (last accessed on 13.06.2022).

Statistical Federal Office. 2021. *Population size Population by nationality and federal states,* available at https://www.destatis.de/DE/Themen/Gesellschaft-Umwelt/Bevoelkerung/ Bevoelkerungsstand/Tabellen/bevoelkerung-nichtdeutsch-laender.html (last accessed on 13.06.2022).

van Rooij, Benjamin, Anne Leonore de Bruijn, Chris Reinders Folmer, Emmeke Kooistra, Malouke Esra Kuiper, Megan Brownlee, Elke Olthuis, and Adam Fine. 2020. *Compliance with COVID-19 Mitigation Measures in the United States.* Amsterdam: Amsterdam Law School Legal Studies Research Paper No. 2020–21. Available at https://doi.org/10.2139/ ssrn.3582626

Appendix 2: Questionnaire of the online survey

The following is the questionnaire that was used in the two online surveys. The questions in italics were only used in the first round of the survey. Items marked with an arrow → were presented or not depending on the answer to the question asked before.

© The Editor(s) (if applicable) and The Author(s), under exclusive license to Springer Fachmedien Wiesbaden GmbH, part of Springer Nature 2023
P. Kirsch et al., *Societal Self-empowerment in Germany*,
https://doi.org/10.1007/978-3-658-40865-7

Sociodemographic issues:

Age: _____

Gender

☐ female   ☐ male   ☐ diverse   ☐ not specified

Education

☐ Without school-leaving qualification

☐ Secondary school diploma

☐ middle maturity

☐ High school diploma

☐ completed vocational training

☐ completed university studies

Are you employed?

☐ yes ☐ no

Professional activity

☐ Full time employed

☐ Part time employed

☐ in education (pupil/student)

☐ currently unemployed

☐ currently on short-time work

☐ currently on short-time work

☐ pensioner / retiree

☐ not employed (housewife*man)

→ If (not) employed, (previously) in which field.

☐ independent farmer

☐ academic free profession (e.g. doctor with own practice, lawyer)

☐ Self-employed in trade, commerce, industry, service, etc.

☐ Civil servant/judge/professional soldier

☐ Employee

☐ Worker

☐ in training

☐ assisting family member

→ If employee

☐ Industrial and plant foremen in the employment relationship

☐ Employees with simple activities (e.g. salesperson, clerk, typist)

☐ Employees who perform difficult tasks independently according to general instructions (e.g., clerks, accountants, technical drafters)

☐ Employees who provide independent services in a responsible capacity or have limited responsibility for the activities of others (e.g., research assistant, authorized signatory, department head)

☐ Employees with extensive management duties and decision-making powers (e.g. director, managing director, board of directors of larger companies and associations)

→ When workers

☐ Unskilled or semi-skilled worker

☐ Skilled worker or skilled laborer

☐ Foreman, column leader, brigadier

☐ Master craftsman, foreman

→ When official

☐ Ordinary service (up to and including head of department)

☐ Intermediate service (from assistant to principal secretary/official inspector inclusive)

☐ Senior civil service (from inspector up to and including Oberamtsmann/Oberamtsrat)

☐ Senior civil service, judges (from government council upwards)

→ **If independent**

☐ no employees

☐ 1 employees

☐ 2 to 9 employees

☐ 10 to 49 employees

☐ 50 employees and more

→ **When academic free profession**

☐ no employees

☐ 1 employees

☐ 2-9 employees

☐ 10 and more employees

How many people live in your household? _____

How many children under 18 live in your household? _____

In which state do you live? _____

1. **How satisfied are you with the functioning of democracy in Germany?**

not at all
satisfied

very
satisfied

2. **In general, would you say that one must always follow the law, or are there situations where one should follow one's conscience, even if it means breaking the law?**

☐ Follow without exception
☐ Following your conscience in exceptional situations
☐ I can not say

3. **When you think about the performance of the federal government in Berlin. How satisfied are you with the way they do their work in the following areas?**

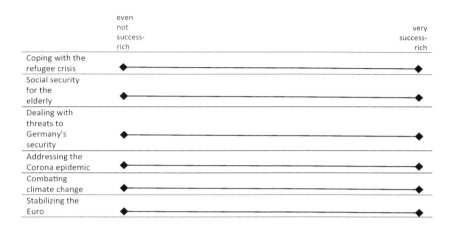

4. **Please tell me how much trust you have in each of the following institutions or organizations.**

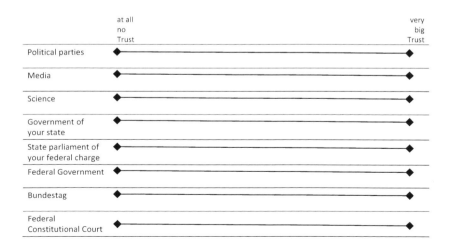

5. **To what extent do you agree with the following statements?**

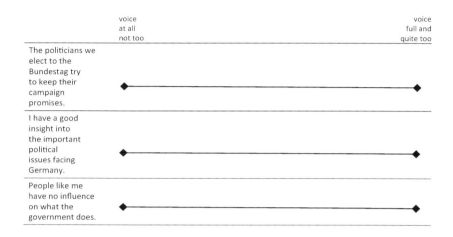

6. **How interested are you in politics?**

7. **In the federal election, you have two votes, a first vote and a second vote. How does that work, which of the two votes is decisive for the distribution of seats in the Bundestag?**

☐   the first vote

☐   the second vote

☐   Both are equally important.

☐   I don't know.

8. **Many students have demonstrated on Fridays as part of the Fridays for Future movement in the past year. Do you find these demonstrations generally right or wrong?**

        ☐ Correct

        ☐ not right

        ☐ don't know

9. **Have you or anyone in your family actively participated in demonstrations of the Fridays for Future movement?**

        ☐ Yes, I myself have participated

        ☐ Yes, someone from my family participated

        ☐ No, neither I nor anyone in my family participated

10. **How do you assess the demonstrations during school time? Do you think that compulsory schooling has priority and that demonstrations should take place outside school time or should demonstrations be held during school time?**

        ☐ Compulsory education has priority

        ☐ Demonstrations should be conducted during class time

        ☐ don't know

11. **It happens that people take the law into their own hands. Do you consider such behavior to be correct?**

        ☐ Yes   ☐ No   ☐ Don't know

12. **In your opinion, how likely is it that in the next two months,**

	at all not probable	absolutely probably	is already happens
you or someone in your family becomes infected with the Corona virus.	◆————————————————◆		☐
You or someone in your family needs inpatient hospital treatment for a corona infection	◆————————————————◆		☐
You or someone in your family dies from a Corona infection.	◆————————————————◆		☐

13. **There were quite a few measures to prevent the spread of the Corona pandemic. Many shops had to close, schools and kindergartens were closed, sports facilities could not be used anymore and one should not meet with people outside one's own household anymore. What do you think?**

☐ Measures were too far-reaching

☐ Measures were just right

☐ Measures did not go far enough

14. **To what extent do you agree with the following statements?**

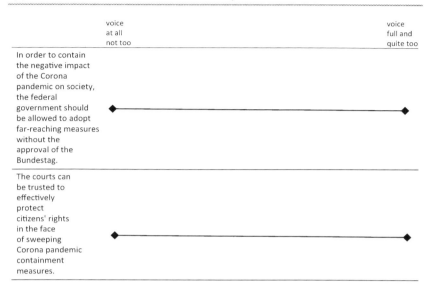

voice at all not too		voice full and quite too
In order to contain the negative impact of the Corona pandemic on society, the federal government should be allowed to adopt far-reaching measures without the approval of the Bundestag.	◆————————————————————◆	
The courts can be trusted to effectively protect citizens' rights in the face of sweeping Corona pandemic containment measures.	◆————————————————————◆	

15. **What do you think: Is the economic damage caused by the current measures to contain the Corona pandemic greater than their benefit to society, or is the social benefit greater than the economic damage?**

The social Benefit is greater as the economic economic benefits	The economic Harm is greater than the societal damage
◆————————————————————◆	

16. **If you're being honest: Have you always followed all the Corona restrictions or have you occasionally done things that you should have avoided, such as meeting friends or going to work even though you could have worked from home?**

☐ always adhered to the restrictions

☐ mostly adhered to the restrictionst

☐ often adhered to the restrictions

☐ sometimes adhered to the restrictions

☐ rarely adhered to the restrictions

☐ never adhered to the restrictions

17. Have you installed the Corona app on your smartphone?

☐ yes   ☐ no

18. → If not

☐ I will certainly still install the app

☐ I will probably still install the app

☐ I will probably not install the app

☐ I will certainly not install the app

☐ I do not own a smartphone or the app does not work on my smartphone

19. How likely is it that you will be caught by the police or the local authorities if you do not comply with the Corona restrictions?

Gar   Not   Very
probable   true-
                                                                     apparent

◆───◆

20. Imagine you had not complied with one of the Corona regulations and had been caught. How bad would that have been for you?

at all   very
not   bad
bad

21. **The restrictions due to the Corona crisis are being evaluated differently. In particular, the restriction of basic rights by the Corona protection measures is being discussed: Some say that these restrictions are necessary to protect the health of the population. Others also have concerns that our basic rights are too severely restricted by the Corona protection measures. What do you think? Do you consider the restrictions on basic rights to protect against the Corona pandemic to be justified or not justified?**

at all   full-
not   come
just-   just-
manufactures   manufactures

22. **If a vaccine against Covid-19 will be available, how likely is it that you will get vaccinated?**

☐ very likely

☐ quite likely

☐ draw

☐ unlikely

☐ Not at all likely

23. **Have you participated in demonstrations against the restrictions due to the Corona pandemic?**

☐ Yes   ☐ No

24. **In politics, people often talk about "left" and "right." Where would you place yourself?**

Left   Right

25. **If there were a federal election in Germany next Sunday, which party would you vote for?**

        ☐ CDU/CSU

        ☐ SPD

        ☐ AfD

        ☐ FDP

        ☐ The LEFT

        ☐ Alliance '90/The Greens

        ☐ Another party: _____

        ☐ I would not vote.

        ☐ I would not be allowed to vote.

26. *26. Which of the following statements do you agree with:*

        ☐ *Laws must be obeyed without exception*

        ☐ *In exceptional situations, one must follow one's conscience and transgress laws*

        ☐ *You only have to abide by the law if the government abides by it.*

        ☐ *You only have to obey laws if you agree with them*

        ☐ *Laws do not have to be obeyed if there are no negative consequences*

27. **Please indicate to what extent you agree with each statement.**

	voice not at all	voice little too	voice something too	voice Quite too	voice fully agree
(1) I am convinced that most people have good intentions.	☐ 1	☐ 2	☐ 3	☐ 4	☐ 5
(2) Nowadays, you can't rely on anyone.	☐ 1	☐ 2	☐ 3	☐ 4	☐ 5
(3) In general, people can be trusted.	☐ 1	☐ 2	☐ 3	☐ 4	☐ 5

28. **Please indicate how likely you find the following statements**

I think,...

(1) ... there are many very important things happening in the world that the Öffentlichkeit is never informed about.

0%	10%	20%	30%	40%	50%	60%	70%	80%	90%	100%
secure not	extremely untrue	Very untrue	untrue	rather untrue	unent- divorced	rather true	true-	very true	extremely true	safe
☐	☐	☐	☐	☐	☐	☐	☐	☐	☐	☐

(2) ... Politicians do not usually tell us the true motives behind their decisions.

0%	10%	20%	30%	40%	50%	60%	70%	80%	90%	100%
secure not	extremely untrue	Very untrue	untrue	rather untrue	unent- divorced	rather true	true-	very true	extremely	safe
☐	☐	☐	☐	☐	☐	☐	☐	☐	☐	☐

(3) ... Government agencies closely monitor all citizens.

0%	10%	20%	30%	40%	50%	60%	70%	80%	90%	100%
secure not	extremely untrue	Very untrue	untrue	rather untrue	unent- divorced	rather true	true-	very true	extremely	safe
☐	☐	☐	☐	☐	☐	☐	☐	☐	☐	☐

(4) ... Events that at first glance *seem unrelated are often the result of secret activities*.

0%	10%	20%	30%	40%	50%	60%	70%	80%	90%	100%
secure not	extremely untrue	Very untrue	untrue	rather untrue	unent- divorced	rather true	true-	very true	extremely	safe
☐	☐	☐	☐	☐	☐	☐	☐	☐	☐	☐

(5) ... There are secret organizations that have great influence on political decisions.

0%	10%	20%	30%	40%	50%	60%	70%	80%	90%	100%
secure not	extremely untrue	Very untrue	untrue	rather untrue	unent- divorced	rather true	true-	very true	extremely	safe
☐	☐	☐	☐	☐	☐	☐	☐	☐	☐	☐

29. **Imagine you have 1000 €. You can invest this by entrusting any amount of it to another, unknown person. You will keep the rest of the money in any case. The invested amount will be tripled. The other person can give you back a part of the tripled money, how much that is, decides the person themselves. So if you invest a lot of money and the other person shares the profit fairly with you, you can increase your money this way. If the other**

person is unfair, you can lose money. How much money would you invest? (0–1000 €)

Response: _____

30. How much do you trust the following information sources?

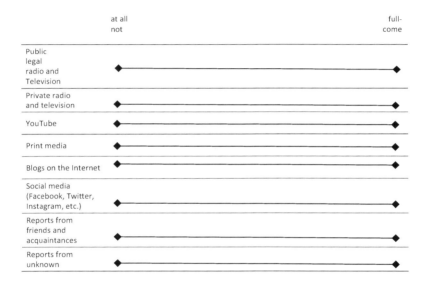

31. *To what extent do the following statements apply to you?*

		Does not apply at all	rather not true	neither	rather true	fully applies
(1)	I am rather reserved, reserved.	☐ 1	☐ 2	☐ 3	☐ 4	☐ 5
(2)	I trust others easily, believe in the good in people.	☐ 1	☐ 2	☐ 3	☐ 4	☐ 5
(3)	I am comfortable, prone to laziness.	☐ 1	☐ 2	☐ 3	☐ 4	☐ 5
(4)	I'm relaxed, I don't let stress get me down.	☐ 1	☐ 2	☐ 3	☐ 4	☐ 5
(5)	I have little artistic interest.	☐ 1	☐ 2	☐ 3	☐ 4	☐ 5
(6)	I get out of myself, I'm sociable.	☐ 1	☐ 2	☐ 3	☐ 4	☐ 5
(7)	I tend to criticize others.	☐ 1	☐ 2	☐ 3	☐ 4	☐ 5
(8)	I complete tasks thoroughly.	☐ 1	☐ 2	☐ 3	☐ 4	☐ 5
(9)	I get nervous and insecure easily.	☐ 1	☐ 2	☐ 3	☐ 4	☐ 5
(10)	I have an active imagination, I am imaginative.	☐ 1	☐ 2	☐ 3	☐ 4	☐ 5

Printed in the United States
by Baker & Taylor Publisher Services